What Would Mary Ann Do?

A guide to life

D0188760

Dawn Wells
with Steve Stinson

Illustrations by James Bennett

TAYLOR TRADE PUBLISHING
Lanham • Boulder • New York • London

Published by Taylor Trade Publishing
An imprint of The Rowman & Littlefield Publishing Group, Inc.
4501 Forbes Boulevard, Suite 200, Lanham, Maryland 20706
www.rowman.com
16 Carlisle Street, London W1D 3BT, United Kingdom

Distributed by NATIONAL BOOK NETWORK

British Library Cataloguing in Publication Information Available
Library of Congress Cataloging-in-Publication Data Available
ISBN 978-1-63076-028-1 (cloth : alk. paper)
ISBN 978-1-63076-029-8 (electronic)

The paper used in this publication meets the minimum requirements of American National Standard for Information Sciences—Permanence of Paper for Printed Library Materials, ANSI/NISO Z39.48-1992.

Printed in the United States of America

What Would Mary Ann Do?
A guide to life

Illustration by James Bennett

To my devoted mother, Evelyn. Your unconditional love taught me Mary Ann values without you ever even knowing it.

To my beloved father, Joe. You gave me love and confidence. I can still hear you saying, no matter what I tried, "Ahhh, you can do it!"

Contents

Russell Johnson

Foreword

We love Mary Ann because she is a useful, enthusiastic force in our lives. She never holds back, never equivocates. When there is something to be done, there she is, pitching in with both hands. We love her because we *like* her.

We love Mary Ann because she is the future, the hope of our world. The youngest of the castaways, Mary Ann has her entire life in front of her. Watching her unfailing good cheer, her optimism is never in question. We love her because we need her emotional support and her belief that all will turn out well.

We love Mary Ann because she is full of love for all. Mary Ann totally accepts not only the situation she is forced to survive, but the people who share her new life. It matters not to her if Gilligan bungles a rescue attempt, if Ginger is more glamorous, if Mrs. Howell is more sophisticated, or if the professor is too shy to act upon his attraction to her. Her love and acceptance are democratic and across the board. We love Mary Ann because we need to be loved unconditionally.

We love Mary Ann because of Dawn Wells. Sherwood Schwartz created *Gilligan's Island* and its inhabitants, but the actors breathed life into their characters. Thus, my dear, dear friend Dawn Wells did so with Mary Ann. Dawn added the flow of love and life to her character and made us love her. Please allow me to repeat: we love Mary Ann because of Dawn Wells.

— *Russell Johnson*

WHAT WOULD MARY ANN DO?

...a
guide
to
life

Hi!
It's me.

They told me, "You should write a book." I said, "I don't want to write a book. I want to talk to you." They said, "Dawn, we can't make that many copies of you."

As we shall see, "they" are usually right. So, I'm writing to you, but I still wish I could be talking with you.

Mary Ann or Dawn?

Now, there's a question. It's usually "Mary Ann or Ginger?"

Every character on *Gilligan's Island* was given a broad "stock" comedy role to fill — captain, mate, wealthy man, wealthy wife, professor, movie star — except one. Mary Ann was not given a character description. She was given a name and location — Kansas farm girl. I had to fill in the blanks. So, from the get-go, the Mary Ann character was different. She wasn't a Hollywood creation. She was molded by me, from me.

I think this is why, over time, as the *Gilligan's Island* reruns multiplied and the Mary Ann phenomenon grew, fans of the show came to see the fictional Mary Ann Summers and the real Dawn Wells as almost the same person.

So, when I say, "Hi, it's me," you might be wondering who "me" is. Well, let's go with what the book cover says, "by Dawn Wells."

Now, I want to talk to you about both of us. I drew from myself to make Mary Ann in 1964. I was 25. I've had a much longer and richer life since the show that I can now share with you. Still, when I think about it, everything I am today was in place then, when I was 25.

At first glance, Mary Ann doesn't seem to fit in this age today, does she? Her manners. Her innate sense of propriety. Her ponytails, gingham dress, and short shorts. Her plainspoken demeanor. Would Mary Ann use emoticons today? I think…
maybe :)

Birth control pills, the feminist movement, and the sexual revolution were barely even known when Mary Ann landed on the island 50 years ago. The whole idea of a "good girl" has evolved — *Gilligan's Island* . . . to *That Girl* . . . to *Dallas* . . . to *Sex in the City* . . . to reality TV . . . you get the idea.

Many a good girl today will publicly say and do things that would have made her *Scarlet Letter* material on the island.

But still, Mary Ann does fit. She fits today just as she fit two generations ago. She fits because she is timeless. The values and principles of her character are timeless. I know this because the core of Mary Ann is really me. I mean, I built her from scratch. You can't ignore it. It's your essence. If you play a character long enough on stage or screen, I think your true self shows through.

I want you to know you are not reading a put-down of Ginger or Tina Louise in any way. Viewers may have thought she was doing a Marilyn Monroe thing. The breathy voice. The eyes. Whatever. If so, she made it look easy and it was impeccably performed.

Tina was perfectly cast. She knew how to play a movie star because she already was one. I was in awe. She had magnificent discipline and she never dropped character. I really think she enjoyed the role.

Let me be the scout. You can be the wagon train.

You hear it all the time lately: "We're in the worst shape since the Great Depression!" Well, I was *born* during the Great Depression. I've been around. I've driven the Road of Life and I started before they had automatic transmissions.

Things haven't changed so much that I can't predict what's coming your way, whether you are 25 or 50. So, I'm inviting you to stick around.

What good is knowing all this stuff if I have no one to tell it to? I've been here for a long time. I've been dating men for forty years. I *know* what I'm talking about. So, let's get started.

I'm not your mother. I'm not a therapist. I'm just…me. In my travels, much of my time is spent talking and listening. And as a single woman, there aren't many places I haven't traveled to. I'll talk to anyone. I even talk to myself. A lot. I do, but so what?

I grew up in Reno, Nevada. It was the opposite of Kansas — gambling, divorce, legal prostitution. My hometown was the divorce capital of the world. People who wanted a divorce would move there for six weeks to establish residency and then get a cheap, fast divorce. Divorce was uncommon everywhere else in the country.

Behind the glitz and the lights and the divorce mills, Reno was actually very traditional and conservative. So, I grew up seeing both sides. My parents were divorced when I was four, but I did not grow up in a "broken home." I was raised by a very good mother and a great dad. My parents remained friends for life and both raised me. I had two families who loved me! My mother was *protective*. I could tell my father *anything*.

So, when I looked out my window, I may not have seen a Kansas farm, like Mary Ann, but when I looked back into the window I saw a lifestyle and values that would be very much at home on that farm.

I was not thin — always one size too big from the seventh grade on. I had acne when I was a teen. I had to hot pack my face with medication every night. My knees started dislocating in the sixth grade, actually in a ballet class. So, no ballet, no sports. And then I got braces on my teeth. In spite of this I was fairly popular and had really good friends.

I learned that the belle of the ball doesn't have to be a belle. I learned that beauty is an illusion. You make the very best of what you have, what you are, and what you can be. I still believe that.

Mary Ann was the most stable of the castaways. Yes, she was a

MARY ANN'S LIST FOR LIVING AND LOVING

It's ok to pull back.

It's ok to be shy.

It's ok to be uncomfortable.

It's ok to want more.

It's ok to experiment and grow.

It's ok to know the person you are with.

It's ok to wait.

It's ok to put yourself out there.

It's ok to have a bad date.

It's ok to keep trying.

voice of reason, but she could also cook, clean, and sew. How did all those single men on the island manage to overlook perfect marriage material?

It's not my ego talking, but Mary Ann wasn't just a silly and sweet ingénue. She was bright, fair-minded and reasonable, and I like to think that's what I brought to her. She was a little more of a Goody Two Shoes than I am. Sherwood Schwartz, the show's producer and creator, was smart enough to put her in short shorts so you wouldn't think of her as your bossy sister. I helped create my own wardrobe from there.

What's changed since Mary Ann was marooned.

First, let's look at what's different. How do I know what's different? I speak to and with groups of young people. Done it for years. What I hear comes unfiltered. When I am in a room with young women and there is no chaperone, I hear what they are really thinking about. They ask me about drugs, sex, religion, everything.

At that age, most of them don't talk to their parents about these things. At least that's the way it seems. It's the age when they are absolutely sure their parents don't know anything. They see me, and they see Mary Ann as a friend who won't judge them, but who is also a role model their parents accept. She's positive.

Here is what they tell me.

They say sex today is different. A kiss was barely allowed on *Gilligan's Island*, much less a view of my navel. Today, sex is everywhere. At least the topic seems to be.

It's the lingerie shop at the mall. It's the magazine cover — make that dozens of magazine covers — at the grocery stores, drug stores, convenience stores, airports. It's the billboard for the x-rated bookstore. Heck, it's the billboard for expensive jeans! It's the erectile dysfunction ads. It's the movies. It's the soap operas. It's *primetime*! Meanwhile, there hasn't been a Mary Ann-style character on the air in forever. There hasn't been a good girl over 14. Sooner or later, a Third Rate World rubs off on you, especially if that's all you know.

THE MARY ANN MESSAGE

By Shira Tarrant, PhD

After fifty years, Mary Ann remains a refreshing change from the worn-out sexual props on TV. In a media saturated world, telling little girls (and the rest of us) that being is sexy is a woman's number one job, she offers a different kind of role model.

Sure, she is sexy. But she is also a moral compass reminding fans that it is okay to speak up and take a stand. She teaches us that we can stay true to our ethics, we can know right from wrong — and that we can rock a cute island outfit while doing it.

Shira Tarrant is professor and pop culture critic in the women's gender and sexuality studies department at California State University, Long Beach

The whole idea of what is actually a date is different. Oh, the roles of women in all aspects of life are not the same as they were in 1964! Those old dating rituals just don't seem to match.

Can you picture a man driving to your home, meeting you with flowers, escorting you to his car, taking you somewhere special and paying for every bit of it until he escorts you home? It's actually easier to picture that in reverse, with the woman doing the heavy lifting.

Communication has changed. I sense there is too much drama out there. It's like your life doesn't have meaning if it doesn't have drama. There is emotion, but the way it is expressed is almost impersonal.

I miss the beautiful language of love. Does anyone really believe you can express it with hashtags and emoticons and tweets? Sonnets, they ain't. Hold it! If I had children, I wouldn't want them saying "ain't." Sonnets they *aren't*.

What a combination. Too much drama and too little meaning.

Drinking and drugs are a different story today, especially drugs, which were barely just visible on the horizon in 1964. Even though they are harder to control, drugs are just like alcohol in one very important way. *They can both make a bad idea seem like a good one.*

Now, there is nothing new about drinking, but there is a huge difference between sipping a Manhattan cocktail and a Sex on the Beach shooter. Sipping creates a very different moment than shooting. Is there anyone who thinks you can have an interesting, intimate conversation and build an enduring relationship around binge drinking?

Today the way you meet people is different. Sure, people still meet through friends and work and church and clubs, but now that universe is vastly bigger through online dating. And, of course, that comes with its own problems.

The way you are remembered is different. In Mary Ann's day you could make a mistake and only a few people knew it, and sooner or later they forgot about it. Today that mistake can be witnessed by countless people online and live there for a very long time. It can grow way beyond your personal life and alter your professional life. It can follow you anywhere.

Ah, but pendulums swing.

Sooner or later it has to swing back. Mary Ann couldn't show her navel on television. Britney Spears made the navel a fashion statement. Today, there isn't much of the female anatomy left to the imagination. After you've shown everything, what's next?

Mary Ann is a state of mind. "Good Girl" is a state of mind. The culture we live in has pretty much left it up to you to decide what you are. The rules aren't defined today. You need to set your own.

And so, I present to you Mary Ann's guide. I'm not here to give you rules. I'm hear to help you make your own. Who knows? *You might find yourself ahead of the pendulum.*

perspective

con • duct

noun

: the way that a person behaves
in a particular place or situation
: the way that something is
managed or directed

identity

PERSONALITY

tone

SELF

mindset

SPIRIT

CHARACTER

ATTITUDE

A moral compass that points in all directions

Wealth without work
Pleasure without conscience
Science without humanity
Knowledge without character
Politics without principle
Commerce without morality
Worship without sacrifice.

— Mahatma Gandhi, "Seven Deadly Sins"

Your tattoo will never look better than it does today. It will grow old on you. Faster than you, really. It will age *on* you, but not *with* you. The image, the picture, the symbol, whatever it is that makes up your tattoo probably won't match the temperament of the you of the future any more than your haircut today would look good on your grandmother.

If age is a pre-existing condition, so is your tattoo. Chances are you will grow weary of it, if you already aren't. Chances are you will ask, "What was I thinking?" So let's ask, why do you regret that lizard on your shoulder? You say it's a butterfly? Oh, dear. By the time you are half my age it will be hard to tell the difference. Like so many things, it was so easy to put on and so hard to take off.

I once worked with a young actor who was habitually late and unprepared. He appeared one day with a new tattoo covering his arm from wrist to shoulder. He expected the director to cover him up. I told him, "You have just limited yourself for life."

Knowing what you are doing and why.

What? It's this way: If you are making your own rules, you live in the world you make. Let's take a look at the world that's been made around you. Hmmm. There's a lot of stupid out there. Stupid is an industry. People make careers out of stupid (I'm thinking sex tapes here). So, what to do?

A friend once defined maturity as knowing what you are doing and why. It was famously put another way — "Know Thyself." The problem here is that the hardest person for you to really know *is* yourself. That's true of just about anyone. If you haven't noticed, there is an entire industry devoted to the problem. After the professional psychiatrists and psychologists, here come professionals *and* amateurs on television, radio, even your family, all ready to tell you what it is that you are thinking and why.

I've always said that you are the first mate of your own ship until you are 21 years old. Then you become captain, an adult equipped for the world. I still think that's true. I know you want to be captain at age 18 or even 13, but take it from me: Wanting it doesn't make it so. I'll grant you this — your job as first mate is much more complicated today than it was for me.

There are so many opportunities for stupid now. No wonder parents feel overwhelmed. You view a TV program that seems safe enough, and *bang*, the F-word fills your living room loud and clear. Meanwhile the kids can even hear it in the next room.

You leave what you think is a mainstream magazine on the table and, *bang*! There's the soft porn image in a clothing ad. At least that's only sexual innuendo. You go to the gym and the step class echoes with sexually primitive rap. At the YWCA!

Music that was vulgar when you were young is playing at the grocery store. On the elevator, cable TV, network TV. There is no way to prepare yourself. You are standing on a corner holding your child's hand when a bus drives by with a larger than life image — two half naked punks and a bikini-clad model with no top. Whoops!

And then there is the internet and your email inbox! And then there are the movies! It crosses all generations. We're all seeing the same things.

These are all pieces of *stupid*. No. That's not it. The problem here is the absence of *don'ts*. Let me hit the pause button here. We need to talk before you drop me into the folder marked "prude."

I love it when people say, "I have made my share of mistakes." *My share*. Like there is a quota. Well, okay, whatever my quota is, I'm sure I probably have made it, although I don't think I've exceeded it.

I've had a marriage end. I've had moments when my good sense abandoned me. If you want to say I have the attitude of a prude, well, I think prostitution should be legal. How's that? I'm not stamping my tiny foot or shaking my finger at you.

23

Now, about Don'ts. Don'ts are the white lines on the road of life. Once you topple a Don't, what do you see in front of you? Another Don't to topple.

Restraint can set you free. I have always been grateful I graduated from Stephens College. It is a small, private women's college in Columbia, Missouri. It is still today a place for women who want to develop an identity as they learn.

Story time! My father didn't really understand why I wanted to go to an all-female college. He thought it would isolate me. It was the opposite. For me, it was liberating. The social rules were hard and fast. By today's standards, though, it was the equivalent of a nunnery. Plus, boys were not a part of your routine day.

With so many distractions out of reach, I was free to use my mind. On the campus. In the classroom. I could be who I wanted to be with no male competition . . . and no competition for males.

I was raised as an only child, and I really liked living with a lot of girls who liked living together. In that atmosphere, you aren't competing for boys. You aren't there to find a husband. You are there to develop yourself. I was there to learn.

It turned out to be the place that opened my eyes to many possibilities. Mary Ann was born there, in a way. I couldn't take physical education because of my bad knees, so I took a drama class instead. My theater professor, Dr. William West, took the time to get to know me. He saw my potential. He said, "Dawn, this is what you ought to do."

At the time, Stephens was a two-year school. After graduation I chose the University of Washington in Seattle because of it's outstanding theater department and pre-med studies. I vacillated between both. I wanted to be a pediatric surgeon. I gave myself two years to decide what to do. In the end, I got my degree in theater and chose Los Angeles as my destination, and never looked back.

If anything goes, what stays?

So, here you are, fourteen, fifteen, sixteen, twenty years old. Maybe you are in college. Wherever you are, you are still the first mate of your ship. You live in a world where a 12-year-old can get her hands on a morning after pill and the parents be damned. You are very much on your own. At the time when you really are least able to, you need to listen to your Big Brain.

Every person has a Big Brain and a little brain (the little brain doesn't deserve capital letters). That's not science, that's just Dawn talking. Or maybe it's Mary Ann. (We could even call your Big Brain your Mary Ann Brain. Hey, I like that.)

When your little brain is in charge, that's when mistakes get made. Your little brain can't stand Don'ts. Can't stand *rules*. Can't stand the word *no*. Your little brain wants and wants and *wants*.

Your little brain thinks that *now* is the right time for everything. Your little brain only understands *now*. Your little brain hasn't a clue what the future is, much less what it means. Your little brain wants to be out of control. Your little brain has no self-respect.

You little brain is a child inside you, no matter how old you are.

Your little brain is shallow. You look in the mirror and your little brain sees a chubby kid with bad skin (I just described myself as a teenager). Your little brain can't see beneath the surface.

Here's the worst part. Just when you think maybe you've got it all figured out, you find that your little brain can take over at any time at any age.

What to do? For me, it started with the debate team in high school. I loved debating and I loved the way the debates were conducted. You had to be prepared to argue both sides of an issue and you were not told which side you would argue until you went to the podium. Your position was given to you at that moment. (Note to self: pray that could happen on cable television.)

This was a life lesson for me. It formed the way I deal with the world. Confront me with a situation and I'll ask, "What's the worst that could happen?" What are the consequences? What is the other half of the story? That's my way of looking at both sides. It is the question your little brain never ever ever ever — whoa, that's three evers — wants to hear.

Your little brain isn't you. Oh, it's partly you, but not the whole you. It's the sum of all the wonderful parts of you.

The whole you is wonderful.
The whole you respects you.
The whole you wants to own what you've done.
The whole you believes you are worth something.
The whole you has standards.
The whole you has Don'ts.

Your Mary Ann Brain directs the whole you. Your Mary Ann Brain knows that something in your past may not necessarily belong in your future. Your Mary Ann Brain understands now, the present, and it understands how now fits into the future.

On *Gilligan's Island*, Mary Ann was often the only person using her Big Brain. Your Big Brain is smarter. It thinks ahead of time. It thinks about consequences. It asks, "What's the Right Thing?" It is ready for the moments that come.

Ahem . . .

Which brings me to sex, like maybe you thought we were just talking about tattoos. The truth is, there is nothing stopping you. I'm talking to you. Yes. You.

The culture I grew up in is gone. This was the culture where you began to have adult impulses at maybe fifteen years old. When I attended Stephens College there were no drugs on campus. Beer was rare and secret. Liquor was forbidden. Dorm hours were controlled. There were standards for behavior on campus.

We couldn't ride in a car with boys the first six weeks. Hmmm, girls, why do think they picked the first six weeks? Could that have been hunting season? We arrived in Columbia on a special Stephens College train.

I boarded the train in San Francisco and watched as we took on more and more new Stephens students all the way to Missouri. By the time we got to Stephens the train was full of girls. And who met the train? Just about every boy from the University of Missouri, which was also in Columbia. Oh, yes, they were *so* ready to help with our luggage.

You couldn't smoke on campus. Church on Sunday? Required. You were in your room after lunch for an hour of study or a nap. We wore hose to dinner. (On those days when hose were uncomfortable, we would take an eyebrow pencil and line our legs to give the appearance of a seam. Hey, we got away with it once in awhile.) It was also a culture where virginity meant something.

The culture you are growing up in is not different, it is *indifferent*. The culture you live in now seems indifferent to your choices. "Go ahead!" "Mom and Dad will never know!" "Here's a pill!" "Take a sip." " Just for tonight!"

Time to call in the Big Brain.

What's the worst that could happen?

I think you already understand pregnancy and disease. There is another result, though.

Every time you engage in meaningless sex you become less human.

Too harsh again? Okay, show me the humanity in it. Show me the affection for you. Show me the beauty in it. Show me the appreciation of you in it. What do you say when you're done? Thanks? Nice job? No regrets? Show me the true intimacy. Where is it? Is it just an exchange of bodily fluids?

Yes, I know about the so-called hooking up trend. It is nothing more than the triumph of the little brain. In other words, it is stupid, shallow, and meaningless (harsh again!). I knew a young man, a college student at a small school just a year or so ago. He gets a call from a girl (note I did not refer to her as a "woman"). She has a date at eight. Can she come over and hook up with him at five?

Great. Just trot on over and do me. Sexuality with no intimacy. Giving your bodies instead of your hearts. Where is the good in it? Then it all ends up on Facebook. There it is, like a tattoo that won't go away.

Are you starting to understand what I meant when I said Don'ts make you free? Can too many choices equal too many regrets? That's up to you because you are on your own. The choices are there. Your parents can't hide them. The culture is too powerful.

I can only offer this: Look for the closest thing to certainty. Where do you find that? Start by considering what stands the test of time. *A long time.* Most people live in the present, have little grasp of the past and are stunned by the future. Try understanding the past and letting it enrich your future. The answers are there. What has always worked? Use your Big Brain.

I hear women even my age and younger marvel at the idea of hooking up. It's so…easy. Talk with them and you can almost see their two brains at play as they think it through. It usually starts off with a tone of jealousy. "Oh, my! If it were only that way in my day." It moves into confusion. "How does it work? What are you doing?" It ends with dismissal. "It's just something I don't need.

It's not...right." They are older. They think it through. They let their Big Brains talk down their little brains.

It's stunning really, the differences of the same physical act. The union of a man and a woman is a phenomenal thing if there is love. Love brings along its emotional friends — caring and affection. It is, in its way, a communication that deepens the connection between two people.

With love, it makes one person of two. The more you give away, the more you get back. Without love, it's all missing. Without love, you have to switch off your humanity. The more you give away, the less you get back. Where is the depth?

It's your heart. Sex is sharing more than your body. I am not preaching that you should be a virgin. That's not my place. I can say, though, that your body and your heart are the most precious things you can give away. Why aren't they sacred to you? Why isn't it an emotional connection? Why isn't it a communication? Why isn't it more than just gratification?

Where's the passion?

You hear about passion a lot lately. You hear, "Follow your passion." Let's not take that too literally. Passion drives many good things. It can motivate you. It can lead you into self-improvement and growth.

It can also cloud your judgment, especially if it involves another person. Passion is invisible, but you can't hide it. It can drive you nuts. Time to call in the Big Brain.

I think young girls need a grownup confidante, someone they trust and who their parents also trust. You need a role model of your choosing, someone you admire. It can be so much easier to discuss things you wouldn't share with a parent. Oh, I do so hope you know someone who has traveled through life and who can listen and who can show you the way and who cares about you.

These are the people who can explain the difference between passion and love.

They know what "the throes of passion" means.

They know what it means to have emotions that are out of control.

They know cultural norms other than the ones you see on reality television — the difference between drama and reality.

These are the people who can tell you *what* you are doing and help you to figure out for yourself *why* you are doing it. I have been this kind of confidante with a dear friend's daughter. Her mother encouraged it.

When she confided in me I made this promise to her: I will not share what passes between us unless it's life or death. I kept my promise.

Mary Ann seems to be that kind of confidante. People confide in me. It just happens. They don't see Dawn. They see Mary Ann and open up. It's happened for fifty years. For me, it has been a window into the minds of many, many different types of people.

There is one thing constant, though. They need to confide in someone they trust. Dawn/Mary Ann seems to be a good listener.

Oh, I do so hope you have someone genuine to confide in, to mentor you. If you're older, I hope you can be that mentor.

Story time! I was at an event in Kentucky. It was a barbeque. I was signing autographs. I was taking a break. A most beautiful young girl sat next to me. She was just stunning, radiant, a man magnet…and about fifteen years old. She was a sweet southern young lady.

Her mother was with her. I leaned over and took the girl's hands in mine and looked into her eyes and I said, "Honey, just say 'no.' You will have everything asked of you. Every man in the world age 16 to 60 will be after you. They can't help it and you aren't sophisticated enough yet to deal with it. One slick guy with a promise can derail your life."

Of course, I threw her for a loop. I signed her an autograph, hugged her and we parted. She waited a while and came back to me and thanked me. Her mother did, too. Sometimes it's nice to be Mary Ann. Her mother could preach that forever and get nowhere, or at least get nowhere until it was too late.

For whatever reason, the young woman listened to Mary Ann, so before we parted again, I added one more thing. I told her that when boys see girls like her, they can't help themselves. *She must be the one doing the thinking when he isn't.* When you are my age, you can say that.

You don't have a back button.

If only! You goof up on your computer. You hit the back button and it goes away. Wouldn't that be just fantastic in life? No such luck.

You hear about people exploring their emotions. Well, hold on. Emotions explore you. Those emotions can make you wish you had a back button. The trick is to have some kind of handle on those emotions, something that alerts you when they are on the way. *Sound the alarm! Here they come!*

First, it helps to know the difference between an emotion and a thought. Here's an example.

A teenage girl sent the son of a dear friend of mine — he was fourteen when this happened — a topless photo of herself. What did he do with it? He showed it to his mother, who called the girl's mother, who confronted the girl. Now, she may resent what he did, but imagine the humiliation if that photo had gone viral. *"Hit the back button! Please!"*

What was that girl thinking? Nothing! She wasn't thinking. Her emotions, her little brain, wanted something — attention, popularity, appreciation, "validation" — who knows? You guess. I can't.

I do know that somewhere, somehow, she got the idea that it was just fine to do what she did. Maybe the idea of self-respect had never been explained to her by her parents. Maybe her parents did explain it, but other forces drowned them out. Either way, her Big Brain was waiting to be released from a coma.

She played a game of High Stakes Stupid. This is a game way too many people think they can win.

My heart goes out to the girl who felt the need to send that picture. It is so easy for a girl that age to be swept up in the moment. She may think she has to do something like that because *everybody is doing it,* whether that's true or not. It isn't easy to navigate a world where all around you and all about you, the idea of a moral compass is deemed silly.

Several years after *Gilligan's Island* was running and the ratings in syndication were still high, I was offered half a million dollars to pose topless in a magazine. (That's $3,734,759.62 today). Imagine for a second what it's like when you show that kind of money to your little brain.

Instantly your little brain starts shopping. *Buying!* Your little brain unearths a long buried list of Things It Always Wanted. Your little brain is traveling. *First class!* Your little brain is launching those projects you've dreamed about. *Even the stupid ones!* Your little brain does backflips. It sets off fireworks. It does Elvis imitations ("Thank yuh, thank yuh vurry mush"). Your little brain is talking to you. "Hey, you don't even have to work for it! Of course! Yes! Where do I sign?"

I turned it down.

They said, "Don't worry, we'll airbrush everything." I said, "What about the photographer? He's in the room with me. His eyes aren't airbrushed. I won't undress in front of someone I don't know.

WHICH ONE ARE YOU?

*Take this true-or-false quiz to see if you are a
Ginger or Mary Ann:*

The Mary Ann quiz

T F
☐ ☐ Your smile is your biggest asset
☐ ☐ You follow your mother's advice
☐ ☐ One is the ideal number of partners for you
☐ ☐ A homemade pie is your idea of a great gift
☐ ☐ The more kids, the merrier
☐ ☐ You can fix anything if you put your mind to it
☐ ☐ A day doing nothing is a wasted one

If you answered true to at least four of the questions,
you're a true Mary Ann.

The Ginger quiz

T F
☐ ☐ You turn heads wherever you go
☐ ☐ The size of the diamond makes the difference
☐ ☐ You trust the opposite sex more than your own
☐ ☐ The mirror is your best friend
☐ ☐ "Me" is your favorite word
☐ ☐ You call a handyman to change a light bulb
☐ ☐ Your favorite book is *Vogue*

If you answered true to at least four of the questions,
you're a star (but you already knew that).

Yes, I guess I could have used the money then. That's a lot to say "no" to. Looking back I guess I could ask, "Would it even matter today?" A photo spread in one issue of a magazine forty-five years or so ago. Would anyone even know today? The answer? Yes. I would.

It just wasn't me. As the captain of my ship, it wasn't the course I set. A bimbo in a boob mag is not what I set out to be, but that's what I would have been. Once you do it, all the money in the world can't change that. For me it would have meant throwing everything overboard and charting a new course to a place I didn't want to go.

It would be 20 years before the back button was invented, but I already knew I didn't want to hit it.

Notoriety is a much misused word these days. It is used as though it means the same thing as "famous." It doesn't mean "to be noted." It means "to be known for doing something bad." Maybe the confusion is deliberate. Being famous for doing something bad or something good or something well. What's the difference?

A politician gets nailed in a sex scandal. Oh, the horror! He apologizes, wife at his side. He made "bad choices." He "disappointed" people. The politician disappears for a bit, usually saying a thing or two about Finding Faith — might even say God — again. He's back within a year with a cable TV deal. He didn't need a back button. He just threw the whole thing to the side.

You watch this again and again and again. He's famous — notorious — you aren't. He's on television. You aren't. He's got the big money contract. You don't. He looks like a winner. You feel like a loser. Oh, my. You are *so* on your own.

Sometimes all we have is words.

At a restaurant in Florida, a waiter recognized me. He was very excited and told our table that his girlfriend was pregnant. I asked him how felt about that, bringing his child into the world with no name. I asked him if he knew the meaning of a bastard child. Did he know how his girlfriend truly felt about that?

It shocked him, not to mention everyone else at the table, but I didn't care. If I'm old enough to be your mother I may as well act like it. About a year later I was in the same restaurant. The waiter approached me. He had married his girlfriend. He said, "Thank you for opening my eyes, Mary Ann."

I don't have all the answers. I'm not a therapist. However, I felt the need to speak up. Frankly, I don't know everything girls should know. How could that be possible? I only know what I know and I hope it's the right thing. All I have to offer is words, but if words can move you further toward your Big Brain, then I'm happy.

I'm like anybody else. Sometimes I react too quickly. I jump to conclusions. I get lost in the moment. I forget to put myself into the other person's place. I make mistakes. I have a little brain, too.

Are you a Ginger or a Mary Ann?

The question comes back to me in a different way. It may as well be Ginger or Dawn?

Mary Ann is bright, cute, friendly, and smart. Mary Ann is curious, kind, sensible, straightforward, and open-minded. Her air of attainability might seem at first like a liability, but it's actually a turn-on to most reputable, dependable guys. It takes work to find the key to her heart, but if the right man does, she'll be totally devoted to him forever. For some, there's nothing sexier.

Ginger is beautiful, and knows how to use her prowess by advertising with her diamonds, tight dresses, and perfectly-done hair. Her motor is always running. She's a trophy, a real showstopper. There's no doubt that any man's arm would be improved by having her on it. Ginger's sensuality is *intense.*

A light went off for me a couple of years ago. I was talking with a group of college students. All female. I posed the question: "Could Mary Ann work today?" I meant, of course, is she relevant? Or is Mary Ann ready for the Museum of Antiquities?

Two girls argued the point. The first was vivacious and talkative. Oh, yeah, she said. Mary Ann was a goner. Silly. Out of date. She was horse and buggy in a jet age. The Mary Ann approach to life had nothing, *nothing* to do with her.

The second girl was quiet. She summed up her argument in a sentence. "There are too many Gingers today."

I'd say *worse* than Gingers. Wannabe Bad Girls. Exhibitionists seduced by the illusion of freedom — freedom from self-censorship, from Don'ts. Celebrities with no talent. Famous for no reason. *Glitz and glamour and no substance.*

I hear people say, "She's testing how far she can go." Really. It doesn't look like a test to me. It looks like she's already there. The scores are in.

On the other hand — a recent University of Michigan study found that men and women lie about their sexual partners. It was eye opening for me. Men overstated their number of partners — on average a hard to believe 32. Women stated their number at an average of eight. These numbers only add up if there is a part of us that wants to be Mary Ann.

A Ginger wants to be loved.
A Mary Ann wants to give love.

39

A Ginger is a taker.
A Mary Ann is a giver.

A Ginger is an opportunist (so are most burglars).
A Mary Ann is scrupulous.

A Ginger builds a façade.
A Mary Ann builds a foundation.

A Ginger wants instant popularity.
A Mary Ann lets the world come to her on her terms.

Your little brain is a Ginger.
Your Big Brain is a Mary Ann.

A Mary Ann understands that we are all alike more than we are different, that we all have needs and insecurities and joys. A Mary Ann understands that we are all connected, that living a good life comes from paying attention to other's needs and insecurities and joys. A Mary Ann gets her joy that way.

I wish you good relationships with your family. I wish you self-esteem. Realistic self-esteem. I wish you constancy — to be able to sift through what is surface and superficial and to arrive at who you really are. I wish you friends and associates who reinforce your constancy, who join you, who won't let you become sidetracked or disillusioned.

MARY ANN'S TERRIBLE TOO'S

Too hasty

Too reckless

Too egocentric

Too indiscreet

Too boorish

Too unthinking

Too careless

Too senseless

Too shortsighted

Too immature

Illustration by James Bennett

continuity

per • sis • tence

noun

: the quality that allows someone to continue doing something or trying to do something even though it is difficult or opposed by other people

TENACITY

resolution

PLUCK

DETERMINATION

If at first you don't succeed, fail, fail again

A pessimist sees the difficulty in every opportunity;
an optimist sees the opportunity in every difficulty.

— Winston Churchill

Deep breath here. This might sting a little. Okay. Nobody is born special. This includes you.

I don't care if you have an IQ of 160, it doesn't mean beans until you use it. I don't care if you are born into great wealth. It has no meaning until you put it to work. I don't care if you have a great voice, it won't sing until you train it.

Now, I know you are important to loved ones. That's not what I'm talking about. I'm talking about the kind of importance we seem to have attached to ourselves just because, well, because we're around. So, how is special possible?

Special is earned.
Special means discipline.
Special means persistence.
Special means work.
It also means talent, but talent may as well not be there without the other three.

Here is what special isn't: It isn't a trophy you get for showing up. It isn't an award you give yourself. It isn't any form of instant fame. You don't get to be the judge of how special you are. You don't get to decide how smart or talented you are. Other people will do that for you.

There is a lot of *special* out there right now. A whole bunch of self-esteem and entitlement that strikes me as phony. Example: While I wasn't looking, "college girls" became "college women." Really? Did everybody just suddenly grow more mature? Something tells me the title was awarded instead of earned. Hey! Everybody gets an upgrade! (Hmmm. Are they still college boys, though?)

I can only speak for Dawn, but it strikes me that this limits genuine accomplishment. Why try to improve if you've already been told you are close to perfection?

So, now that I've said you aren't that special, I'm telling you that you can be. The best part about this is that it is very, very, very (three veries!) difficult. Maybe we should call this "The Road to Special."

So, how do you become special?

You fail and you make it work for you. Looked at properly, failure is something to be achieved.

Failure is the road to growth and persistence is your vehicle. Failure teaches you. You've heard of the lubricating product called WD-40. The name stands for "water displacement, fortieth try." There were 39 failed WDs before we got the 40 that is now a household name.

Failure builds character. What matters is what you do after you fail. Babe Ruth struck out 1,330 times, but we only remember his home runs.

Get this: Ruth isn't even in the Top 100 in strikeouts for major league batters. Take a look at who's on the list of all-time strikeouts and you'll see a Who's Who of the best batters in baseball history. What did they have in common? They shook off each strikeout and came back for more.

Everybody thought *Gilligan's Island* would fail, that it wouldn't make it through a season. Sherwood Schwartz didn't care what everybody thought. The critics savaged us the first year. He stuck with the show. It found an audience and became a TV phenomenon. In 2014, the show is still on the air. Fifty years later! Generations later! (Did somebody mention the show has been translated into multiple languages?)

Story time! The phenomenon made things a little easier for me. Roles weren't flying in over the transom, but I didn't have to struggle to make my name known. My work was known. Still, long after Gilligan was a distant line item on my resume, I had to spend *two years* chasing a stage role.

I saw Tyne Daly in *Love, Loss, and What I Wore* off-Broadway and instantly knew I wanted to do that show. It's mostly a series of monologues with an ensemble cast of five women. It's a fabulous play written by Nora and Delia Ephron. A great script and a great director, Karen Carpenter.

When I approached Tyne at curtain call, she remarked, "You

should do this show." I wrote the producer. Nothing. I wrote her again. Nothing. After six months, my agent contacted her. Nothing. Three months later and every three months after, my agent kept trying. Nothing. Nothing. Nothing. After two years, I got the call. I did the show in Chicago in 2011. It was two years and five productions after my first query.

I am persistent. I always want my next role to be a stretch. I understand that I am never near the performance level I want the first time.

I always want to improve.
I always want to work at the next level.
I never want to say, "Now, I'm there. I've achieved it."

You must always try to improve. Analyze your growth.

It's a question of who you are. In America, being a loser is a choice. Yes, it is. It is still the Land of Opportunity. Ignore the ones who say it isn't. Never, and I mean *never*, listen to someone who thinks you can't do it because *they* can't do it.

The most demanding teachers, the toughest coaches, the challenging friends — these are the people you want in your life. These are the people who will help you get the most out of you. They can't help, though, if you don't first believe in yourself and what you do.

When you fail, ask yourself why. Was I not good enough or was I just unprepared? Was I unqualified? Did I work hard enough? What did the failure teach me?

There is no such thing as perfection.

I think overcoming adversity makes you a better person. Weight lifters "achieve failure" by doing repetitions until they can no longer lift the weight. Achieving failure makes them weaker today and stronger tomorrow.

You won't lift that extra weight, though, if you think you are done. "Okay, I am as strong as I'll ever be. Quitting time!"

You won't get better at the keyboard if you stop practicing the piano. If you learned "Chopsticks" at eight years old, that — and only that — is what you'll be able to play when you are 80 years old.

The perfect life is unattainable. Let me try that another way. A perfect life includes imperfection. That's still not it. Try this: There *is* such a thing as perfection. It is failing before succeeding. Really, that's what it is, isn't it?

Life isn't an uphill climb.
It is peaks and valleys.
It is joy and sorrow.
It is laughter and tears.
It is lived in the moments.
It is failure and renewal.
Failure is what makes success sweet.
You will never experience any of them if you don't get in life's game and play it.

Pause button here. Okay, I know those are clichés. You could print them on those little gift shop hand towels. Doesn't matter. They are true. *End pause.* That's why teachers and coaches are good for you. Like my friend, the coach, says, "Always suit up. Never give up." He also said, "The harder I worked, the luckier I got."

If life isn't an uphill climb, then what is "the daily grind?" What does it mean when people describe their lives as "same old, same old?" To me it means they have chosen a level and stopped there. The drive is gone. The desire to improve is gone. "This is as good as it gets."

Funny how that is. We don't admire people who stop. We always want more from them. What's the next Stephen Spielberg movie? Where's the next Apple device? What will J.K. Rowling write now?

If you want to equate perfection with success, here is a definition for you: Success is like climbing stairs. When you get to one level, you look for the next. You take the step. You look for the next. You take the step. You never stop climbing.

You define it.

On graduation day, the students at a school will select the classmate who is "Most Likely to Succeed." (Do they still do that?) Usually this translates as "Most Likely to Get Rich."

Well, what does that mean? Answer: Whatever you want it to mean. Take out a clipboard and ask a hundred people this question: "How much money is enough money?" You will write down a hundred answers.

That isn't what we are up to here. I am not putting any "This Way" signs on the Road to Special. You choose. You define what the goal is. I am telling you, though, that when you get to the goal, you might just see . . . another goal.

You only get out what you put in.

Success really starts with a decision, especially in America. Here, you can actually decide what it is you want to be or do. After that, it's up to you. There's the rub. You won't be or do much just by deciding. You have to try. I think you have to be stubborn.

You learn this right off the bat in show business. It isn't easy to keep believing in yourself when the struggle never stops while the rewards never seem to arrive. It is easy to forget the hardest part of any career is breaking in — when you don't get the part again and again and again.

Story time! When I was in college, I thought long and hard about entering the Miss Nevada contest. The Soroptimist Club of Reno asked me to enter. At the time I didn't know why. I'm not a classic beauty. I considered the Miss America Pageant to be a beauty contest. It isn't. It's a person contest. What kind of person you are — your intelligence and your ability to be a lady. You need much more than beauty. The prizes provided college scholarships.

I agreed to enter. To me, it was experience and training. I was a theater major so I wanted to see if I could perform a dramatic scene in front of an audience. During the question period, my question was: What did I look for in a husband? I told them the truth (the answer is in Chapter 4). I won.

The next step — the Miss America Pageant — is the big show. Fifty girls and a live television show. You have to learn the routines and hit your marks for the camera. It is a lot of work. And we were chaperoned every second. I laugh when I think that today we would call the show "natural." No hair dye. No falsies.

The girl with the best attributes — beauty, talent, manners, bearing, confidence, intelligence — won. I wasn't the winner, but I put all I had into it and left happy.

Was it experience? Was it training? Lessons learned? Was it worth it? Yes, and for the strangest reason. Every time you do a new show you learn something. You polish a talent. That's built in. The single best stage experience I got from the Miss America Pageant was that it improved my ability to center myself. How?

The question and answer part of the contest is a dead serious matter, as is the personal interview with a judge. My session occurred during a breakfast meeting with one judge and three to five contestants.

When I looked up at the judge, while he was seriously asking questions, I saw that he had little pieces of egg in his beard. There they were, bouncing around as he talked. Did I mention this wasn't a laughing matter? I really can't describe what a distraction that was.

I couldn't take my eyes off them. I guess the judge just thought I found him interesting, which I guess I did. After that one, I was confident I could perform in a hurricane.

The fuel of defeat.

If you put negativity and fear into your life, that's what you'll get out of it, too. Same with joy. You are the captain of your ship. It is up to you.

Defeat makes me angry. It's not a bad thing. I use it. It motivates me because I know where to put the anger. It's fuel for my inner fire. I have lost roles to other actors. I didn't like it, but I didn't start disliking the actor, too.

I never blame others, even after circumstances are unfair. When you do that, it's your little brain talking. Dealing with unfairness is just another part of life. Unfortunately, it is routine, so deal with it. Make it work for you.

You, and only you, are responsible for your thought processes, no matter where you come from or where you are. Nelson Mandela said, "Resentment is the poison you give yourself thinking it will kill your enemies."

Oh, easy for you to say . . .

Right now you may be thinking, "Well, Dawn, who says you're so special?" The answer is, "Not me."

I still haven't done Broadway. I never got to be a ballerina, which is what I longed to do. I fell flat on my face doing *Swan Lake*. I mean that literally. I hit the ground. My knees aren't dancer's knees. Shoot, they barely qualify as walker's knees.

Also, I probably would never have gotten down to that ballerina size two, anyway.

I have been on stage constantly for fifty years and I am still striving to be better. I haven't done half the roles I want to do. There has never been a time when I didn't want to do more and be more. And learn more.

I think I was lucky to get in a show that became famous, but I wasn't lucky to get in the show. I was ready for it. I was trained in theater. I looked at the odds. At that time the only real options were New York and Los Angeles. The odds of getting a role in New York were lower. It was mostly musicals and I don't sing. (Ugh, more on that, later.)

I made a deliberate choice to be in Los Angeles. I didn't just show up in L.A. wanting to be a movie star. I wanted to work.

Most importantly, I auditioned. I "showed up" so to speak. I had given myself a time limit. If I didn't make it after one year in Hollywood, it was back to med school. (I still wonder about that. I think if genetic medicine had been around then, I might be a doctor doing community theater today.)

I think my background in science helped me. I had a plan. I was prepared. This kind of analysis can be hard for people in the arts. You have to put aside your emotions. At any given time, I could — and still can — only be the best that Dawn Wells can be. It's a matter of me knowing me. I knew me. I was naïve, but not so naïve as to think I truly understood Hollywood. That I had to learn.

I got a stage role at The Music Box theater the first week I was there. I was in *Black-Eyed Susan* with Mercedes McCambridge and Leon Ames. The theater paid for my equity card. I'm pretty sure that's a card that is harder to get today.

So I went to work as a pro right away. This might seem like a Hollywood fairy tale — ingénue sweeps into town and is discovered — the kind that fuels illusions of quick stardom.

I got the role because I had four years of training for the stage and two college degrees. (You never stop training.) So many young women show up in Hollywood today wanting to be in the movies, but have no training. It can work, but the odds aren't as good.

It's about taking the shot.

After an audition, there can be a zillion reasons for rejection. You can be the wrong type. You can be too short or too tall, too young or too old (I will never be picked for a blonde, blue-eyed Swedish family). I can only get so thin. It is what the director needs, assuming you are the best you can be. That's up to you.

It's the same in life. If you fear an audition, if you fear showing up, if you fear putting yourself out there, then you aren't fully ready for life any more than Babe Ruth would be ready for baseball if he feared the batting box.

The auditions don't stop at one. You will be asked again and again to prove yourself, to demonstrate that you've got what it takes. If you genuinely strive to succeed, you will be rejected more than you are accepted. Just like The Babe's strikeouts. If you fear the audition, it really means you fear the opportunity.

This kind of fear is your little brain talking to you. Oh, there is Big Brain fear. I mean, you just don't go sailing in a hurricane. Little brain fear, though, incapacitates you. Your little brain is that voice telling you, "Don't even try." Then, your little brain envies the people who did try. Your little brain tells you, "It's not worth it." Then your little brain envies the people who reap the rewards of effort. Ugh. Your little brain.

The worst trait of the little brain is false confidence. It does this by belittling the accomplishments of others. "Hey, anyone can do that." Funny, isn't it, how your little brain manages to keep you from actually putting your confidence to the test? Hmmm.

A good review can hurt you more than a bad one.

It ain't all glamour and lights. Hold it, I thought I stopped saying "ain't." Okay, that's the last one. *Promise.* It's not all standing ovations. In my business, you get reviewed. There is a lot to be learned from being reviewed. You can learn a lot about yourself. I think it would be great if all professionals would be reviewed for the world to see routinely.

People in entertainment often say they don't read reviews. I am the opposite. I read them. I even like to meet the critics. I think it's a growth process.

When you put yourself out there, on stage or screen, you've opened yourself up to reaction, and let me tell you, the critics don't hold back. Who are the critics?

On the road, especially in smaller venues, the reviewer might be a veteran of the theater or a sportswriter who just wanted the tickets. Both have the power of their publication in pretty much equal measure. In other words, the critic is an influential anybody.

Meanwhile, the cast and I can do a show every night for a week and have seven different nights. The reviewer is there only once. And people talk about unfairness. Please . . . it's all part of the game. We are human. We are part of the team. Part of the whole. Getting every person on the team performing at a hundred percent is a magic that doesn't happen.

People don't exit office cubicles at the end of the day to the sound of applause or boos. They don't read in the next day's news that they flopped or they brought the house down.

Who are your critics?

Why am I talking about reviews? Because everybody gets reviewed. It may not be applause and boos, but you are reviewed nonetheless. This is tricky territory. Your critics could be people who love you or people you have barely met.

Many a fabulous success story begins with the hero ignoring the disapproval of friends and family. Many a tragedy begins the same way.

There are two nevers with critics. Never react emotionally to a bad review. Analyze it and think about it. Same with good reviews. Never believe anyone who says you were perfect. That review that can hurt you, too. It is too easy to believe because you really want to.

There goes your little brain again! It wants praise, admiration, rapture! Applaud me! Oh, the longings too deep for tears.

You have to avoid that. I have always been very critical of myself. Whatever I do, I know I can do it better. It's a message I give myself.

Your Big Brain is your best critic. Your Big Brain knows if the thumb sign should be up or down for you. Your Big Brain knows what you deserve. It knows how much effort you really put into the task.

You will be judged.

Your work gets reviewed. Maybe it's your boss. Maybe it's your customers. In many ways, these are the simplest. If the demands and goals and expectations are clear, then it isn't very hard to tell if you met them.

Your friends review you. Your relatives review you. These can be the most complicated because there is too much room for emotion on both sides. Why is there too much emotion?

Friends and family, especially family members, often form a mental picture of you that gets locked in early. Throw in a bunch of pop psychology and, voila, they think they know you. To them, it means they can judge you.

I've seen it. I'm pretty sure you have, too. Maybe you've done it. Usually, it's the responsible young adult whose parents persist in judging her by her teen behavior. It's worse, though, when you are judged by friends and family who don't understand failure. They see you fail once and that's enough for them. Here's the problem: Sometimes the judgments they lock in are correct.

That's when you are on your own. Just remember, if you see only the certainty of success and they see only the certainty of failure, you are both wrong.

What to do? How about calling in your Big Brain? Your Big Brain will tell you if you are chasing rainbows. It will tell you if you've given everything you have to give, that you left nothing on the table. Your Big Brain will tell you if you are faking it. If your Big

Brain tells you that, then you will be at peace with your performance.

I consider myself lucky. As a child I was told to never eat chocolate. Why? I had terrible acne. Worse, mom shopped for my clothes in the "chubby" section at the store. Let's not forget the braces on my teeth. Ooh.

I was never told, though, that I was ugly. I was never told that I was incompetent. I was never called lazy. I was always surrounded by love and belief in my worth. I don't care how old you are, I truly, deeply hope that you had, or have, good parents.

It is the duty of parents to see the worth in their child and make it known. Remember what I said about reviewers. Some are much better at it than others. Some take the trouble to make themselves better.

I have known women who never escaped a terrible childhood. For them, the insecurity never goes away.

If I am talking about you now, I wish I had a magic formula to help, but I don't. I can only tell you that you don't have to let life's reviews hurt you. They can work for you. Make it the fuel for your inner fire.

When you are on a path of your choosing and your Big Brain tells you it is the wrong one, take a different path. It is never too late. It is *not* the same as quitting.

Story time! I've only gotten one really bad review. It was in San

A GUY WHO WOULDN'T STOP

Alan Hale was even bigger in person than he appeared on television.

One day, he was filming a scene on the *Gilligan's Island* set that involved him climbing up a tree.

The crew put a mattress under him, just in case. It was, after all, a fake tree.

The Skipper was supposed to grab a bird's nest at the end of the limb. The limb broke and he fell out of the tree at ten feet — about the height of a basketball rim. He missed the mattress and landed on cement.

Alan brushed himself off and finished the take and went on to complete the full day's filming. After his fall, he was his usual jolly self. Alan never said a word about it.

The next day he showed up with a cast on his wrist. He had broken it in the fall. Now that, ladies and gentlemen, is *perseverance*.

Francisco. There was bad blood before the curtain went up. The reviewer had been booted from the theater and banned by the owner. This was his first time to be allowed back in.

We were doing a Neil Simon play. The reviewer disliked plays by Neil Simon. The show was a musical. My first. The sound guy was new. Well, not new. He had only done rock concerts. The show was indeed a mess. It was awful. We couldn't hear each other across the stage, let alone the orchestra. The critic just savaged the show and me, but I wrote him a note. I told him I was sorry he had such a terrible evening. I thanked him. What did I thank him for? His honesty and integrity. After he received the note he actually wrote me back. The man was astounded, to say the least.

He wrote, "Every person to whom I have shown this letter is astounded. The next time you're in town, I would be delighted to see your performance. I have never been thanked for a negative review."

Story time . . . again! I was once riding in a car with Clive Barnes, the dance and theater critic for the *New York Times*. How, I wondered, does one become a critic? Clive gave me a long, almost weary look. "After you have seen *Hamlet* forty-two times," he said, "you just know a good one when you see it." From his look I understood that's when you can become a critic — *if you still want to.*

One sign of success: humility.

Ego and self-confidence are two different things. They are often confused. Boy, do I know this. Anybody who actually says what they think knows this, too. I say what I think because I've taken the time to examine what I think. The reaction sometimes? "Who are you to say that?" The answer: Me.

Saying what you really think isn't all that popular. It is misunderstood. Sometimes it looks to me like the truth is considered, well…harsh. It should be told with good intentions. It should be told in a positive tone. It should be told in an appropriate moment. Constructive criticism.

Ambition can be a real negative. You can lose the sense of where you are. It can get to be All About Me. This is the tricky part. Success usually involves leadership. It can be lonely. You have to balance All About Me (your little brain) with All About the Job (your Big Brain). You have to balance these.

Maybe you've heard of actors who are "difficult." Well, they can be. Some are difficult for the right reasons. Some for the wrong reasons. A star shoulders the burden of a show. Her name is on it. Whether she likes it or not, the public will think it's All About Her. So, she must demand the best from everybody concerned, which is a lot of people.

She must set a standard of excellence for herself and expect everyone else to meet theirs. Those are the Big Brain reasons.

On the other hand, an actor can show up late again and again. She can be unprepared. She can have pointless hissy fits. She can derail a show. That's her little brain talking.

Humility engages your Big Brain. It gives you perspective. Some of the most successful people I know are humble. Humility refreshes you and the people around you. It brings out the best in people. It keeps them coming back.

Nobody wants you when you're down and out.

They don't. Ask yourself, what do you do when you find yourself in the presence of constant complainers? I get out as fast as I can. Trouble is, there is a cottage industry out there telling you that Life is So Hard. The inequality! The glass ceilings! The burdens of life, family, men! *Woe is us!*

Helen Gurley Brown described her early career self as a mouse in a man's world. She worked longer hours. She did the jobs nobody else wanted to do. She demanded more of herself. She didn't meet the company's expectations. She met hers.

When the moment came, she was ready. She saved *Cosmopolitan* magazine. (She turned it into a sex manual, but she saved it.)

She could have succumbed to self pity. She could let her little brain call the shots. But she didn't. Ultimately, she got to call *all* the shots.

What would Mary Ann do?

She'd soldier on. She'd carry more than her weight and smile about it.

She would know that each day offers you the choice of living through a good one or a bad one.

She'd put her yesterdays in the rear view mirror and focus on what's in front of her.

She'd see the Road to Special. She may not be sure she can get to Special, but she wants to be on that road.

I don't care how old you are, there is time for persistence. You can accomplish almost anything if you stick with it and live it.

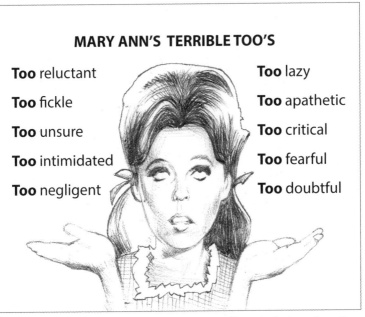

MARY ANN'S TERRIBLE TOO'S

Too reluctant

Too fickle

Too unsure

Too intimidated

Too negligent

Too lazy

Too apathetic

Too critical

Too fearful

Too doubtful

Illustration by James Bennett

MARY ANN'S SELF- ESTEEM TEST

Take the quiz to rate your level of self-esteem and hear what kind of advice Mary Ann has for you.

When you see someone you're interested in at a party, you:
- ☐ A. approach and put your number in his or her pocket
- ☐ B. arrange to be introduced
- ☐ C. leave it to fate

Before you head to a restaurant to dine alone, you:
- ☐ A. dress to the nines
- ☐ B. put on a sensible suit
- ☐ C. dress to disappear

At your 20th high school reunion, you're:
- ☐ A. happy to show who you are now
- ☐ B. hoping your old sweetheart is eating his or her heart out
- ☐ C. praying people remember you

As a single parent back on the dating scene, when you meet someone new, you:
- ☐ A. play it cool
- ☐ B. reveal who you really are
- ☐ C. hide your children at all costs

When you're going on a blind date, you:
- ☐ A. leave it to chance
- ☐ B. Google your date
- ☐ C. peek out the window when the person arrives

On a first date, I would go this far:
- ☐ A. a handshake
- ☐ B. a goodnight kiss
- ☐ C. a one-night stand

When getting to know someone new, you:
- ☐ A. stay as secret as a CIA agent (let him or her do the work)
- ☐ B. act like an interrogator
- ☐ C. tell your whole life story

When you're not interested in someone, you:
- ☐ A. say it gently but clearly
- ☐ B. try one more time
- ☐ C. stop returning the person's calls

When you are interested in someone, you:
- ☐ A. become your best self
- ☐ B. act more distant than you did on the first date
- ☐ C. become to needy to know his interest

If you answered mostly As:
Mary Ann says: You're not intimidated by circumstances and always view yourself as an equal. Not afraid of new experiences, you'll find something of value about the person or evening even if there's not going to be a second date. It's wonderful that you can make the best of everything and find the good in everyone. Just be aware that not everyone is as confident as you, so develop your nurturing and patient side.

If you answered mostly Bs:
Mary Ann says: You're not sure what you need at this moment but are very much open to love. You might have just come off a difficult divorce or just lost the one you love and are regaining your footing. As you continue to search, be cautious and don't rush your feelings. Take your time. Start with friendship without worrying about whether the end result will be a relationship. That way, whatever happens, you'll get a positive outcome.

If you answered mostly Cs:
Mary Ann says: It's all very new and a little intimidating for you. You're not alone! It's fantastic that you're eager to learn, and it's okay if you're still a little shaky. Don't be so quick to pair up. Instead become part of a group where the focus is not on any one person but on the event. There is strength in numbers, so if you are a little insecure someone else can do the talking for you. Freed from pressure, you might find someone you have a lot in common with and the confidence to be yourself.

gentleman

man

noun

: an adult male human being
: a man or boy who shows the qualities (such as strength or courage) that men are traditionally supposed to have

FATHER

HUSBAND

BROTHER

beau

Son

boyfriend

dance partner

I love men

It's not the men in your life that matters. It's the life in your men.
— Mae West

I do love men. Don't get me wrong. I love women, too. It's just that men are different creatures. I am amazed at the differences. They approach things — make that *all* things — from their own perspectives. I do think men are a necessity. I even like to watch a man shave.

There are voices out there saying you can live without them, you should live without them, you should not *want* them.

Oh, really? Well, fine. Go ahead. Sure, you can get along without one. That just leaves more men for the rest of us. Hey, we have a responsibility as women to share the planet. Men are part of it. I'm sharing. You don't have to *need* a man. At my age, if I chose a man based on need, I'd marry a masseuse. (Hey, it used to be a piano player.)

I would sometimes rather spend an evening with a man than with women. Don't get me wrong. I believe in sisterhood. I just don't want their point of view as the main course all the time.

As a group, men seem more alike than they are different. They all have pride and ego to different degrees, of course, but there is something in a man's nature that makes him want to be productive.

I don't think of men as the enemy. I do think of the right man as an asset.

That's what is so great about the time we live in. You get to pick the asset. You live in a time that allows you to be independent. Being independent, though, doesn't isolate you. It's the opposite. The more independent you are, the better partner you become in any relationship. You have more to offer and you have a better grasp of what is offered to you.

Men are more black and white. And thank heaven. They don't talk everything to death. (Note to self: remember that one.) What does this mean? You have to learn to talk to and *with* men. Enough with the gripes about how he doesn't listen! *Maybe you should try saying it in a listenable way.*

Really, how simple is this? If he doesn't listen to you, what's the point in continuing to communicate in the way you do? If you have a target and you miss every time you throw something at it, you need to work on your throw, not the target.

Meanwhile, there are forces at play that want to meld us into a single sex. Funny, it seems to be mostly women who push the issue. You don't think so? Try this: Put a woman in a jacket, pants and necktie. Put a guy in a dress. Which one is cross dressing?

I know a lot about men.

How do I know so much about men? For fifty years, men, total strangers, have confided in me. They talk to me. They are open because they aren't being judged. They tell me things that they might say to a brother or best friend. They confess. They are talking to a friend. They are talking to Mary Ann.

They were 14-year-old boys when they came home from school and watched *Gilligan's Island* reruns in the afternoon. Some were latchkey children and we were their family.

That man-defining question "Ginger or Mary Ann?" didn't come from the original show. It came from the reruns. It came from the 14-year-old boys who are now 40. I still get hundreds of fan letters every month. Men come up to me and tell me, "You were my first crush" or "I married a Mary Ann" or "I'm looking for a Mary Ann" or my favorite, "You're still hot."

If you are in television reruns for fifty years, you don't age there. It leads a parallel life. For some men, I became a sex object frozen in time.

A man approached me a few years ago at a performance site. He told me, "When I was twelve, I couldn't sleep after watching you on television." What a sweet gentle way for a 12-year-old to express himself. Here's another one I've heard: "You got me through puberty in the nicest of ways."

I visited the Pentagon a few years ago. I found myself surrounded by 4-star generals, a sea of military uniforms. They all wanted to tell me about their crushes on Mary Ann. What a pleasure. I was their first love, even if it was a television fantasy. I "raised" a lot of heroes.

Story time! Once, on a long flight, the man in the seat next to me opened up about his life. He had a mistress. He loved his wife and would never leave her, but he had a mistress. He loved his kids, but he had a mistress. I'm pretty sure he never told that to anyone else, at least until he was caught.

I've dated men for forty years. I travel often. I perform on stages across the country. Men try to pick me up. Yes, even at my age. It comes with the territory. They aren't necessarily after Dawn. They want Mary Ann. Years ago, I was on location with a rogue who was after me every second. He wasn't successful (with *me*, ahem). At the wrap party, he stopped everything and announced to the whole group, "Dawn, I give up. I have never been turned down with such class and aplomb. I quit." That kind of thing was rare for me in Hollywood. I haven't been propositioned very often there. Nobody has really gone over the top with me there. I think it's because of the way I handled myself. And there is respect there, both ways.

Story time! My father was part owner of the Thunderbird Hotel in Las Vegas. Show business people were routine at the hotel. When I first moved to Hollywood, a famous, older Broadway producer who was an acquaintance of my father offered to escort me to a party or two in Hollywood. My father thought of him as a chaperone and he was a perfect gentleman.

So, I would show up on his arm at parties. That was it. It didn't take long for me to figure out, though, that there were other girls on the arms of other older men at these parties. They were all knockouts. It didn't take long to figure out that they *weren't* being escorted by perfect gentlemen.

ONLINE DATING
Comparing the profiles of Mary Ann and Dawn Wells

 Islandsweetie64   **Friendlystar22**

Looking for: someone dependable, loyal, and kind, with a sense of humor. He would make a good dad whether he had children or not

Looking for: an intelligent man who is a good listener and makes me laugh, but most importantly, shows kindness and respect to everyone

Pet Peeves: phonies, blowhards, overbearing types, lazy bums, or those lacking responsibility

Pet Peeves: rudeness, vanity, and a bad attitude

Deal Breakers: guys who go for the Ginger type

Deal Breakers: infidelity, superficiality, and self-absorption

Over the Moon for: the professor

Over the Moon for: a guy with good values and high standards

Favorite Date: a picnic, or fly-fishing

Favorite Date: a romantic evening with a nice meal, slow dancing, champagne, and love

Favorite Foods: any vegetable so long as it's fresh, lobster, or a good steak

Favorite Foods: roasted wild duck and real wild rice

Hobbies: baking the most delectable coconut cream pies

Hobbies: painting, reading, watching football, and listening to the news

The Best About Me: my optimism, caring nature, sense of humor, and love of animals

The Best About Me: my ability to connect with people

I went to my father and told him I did not want to do it anymore. I was uncomfortable. The situation was too easy to misinterpret. Done. I knew I might be tossing aside opportunities. I was hobnobbing with the kind of people who can make or break an entertainment career. And I was so young! It wasn't worth it. The perception. The image. To the naked eye (no pun intended) I looked no different than all the other girls. You might say I was learning to Turn It Down before It Comes Up (pun intended).

Men have little brains, too.

Oh, boy, do they! Now, you don't really need to know that much about the way a man's little brain works. It works just like yours, only it responds to different things. A look across the room can light up a man's little brain. A touch on his arm, a husky laugh, a whiff of perfume and his little brain starts making noises like one of those old French taxis.

A man's little brain can confuse *friendly* with *fire*. A man's little brain wants it all to happen *now*. The only reason a man can tell you "This isn't a one-night stand" is because his little brain doesn't even know there is a tomorrow. It isn't hard to see a man's little brain at work. Spinning! It's like a gerbil on a wheel. A man's little brain is his personal, internal con man. It's a card shark. It does Elvis imitations ("Hullo, darlin'"). Here is where we need to do some math. One little brain plus another little brain equals… zero. That's right. If one person isn't thinking, nobody is thinking.

Size matters.

Sizing them up, that is. Judging from the television commercials, you'd think football fans — a.k.a. American men — consist entirely of dolts who require only erections and tires with their beer to make their lives full! You'd think that a man's attention span is four hours. After that, he needs to consult his doctor.

It's way more complicated than that. My father once said to me, "You don't know what boys are about. They don't have to be heroes. Treat them as people." Translation: If you look for handsome, you'll find it, but that might be all you'll find. What do you look for? How about responsible, kind, productive, fun, smart, sincere, and polite? I look for a sense of humor, a listener. I look for a man who can carry his own weight, which instantly rules out drunks and druggies. Give me a man as sensitive as he is strong, as kind as he is tough. Give me man who can be a good dad.

How do you know he is who he says he is? It's easy to be fooled. Personally, I want to see your eyes and hear your voice if you are flirting with me. I want to look at you and see which brain is at work. Do *not* text me and ask me out. Speak to me.

Things are different for women today, you say? Well, yes, and I've enjoyed the benefits. Here's a Hollywood perspective. When Ida Lupino directed *Gilligan's Island* episodes in the sixties, she was among the first female directors, ever. She was certainly the first woman I ever worked with on camera. It was a big deal. Today, women are directing, producing, and winning Academy Awards. So, if women today have the capacity and ability and opportunity to go anywhere, they aren't really competing in a man's world anymore, are they? But what world are they competing in? A world where we're all the same? I don't think so. I hope not.

Women are different from men. Do I really have to point that out . . . again? There is nothing wrong about being different. It's how you express it, and that really separates the Mary Anns from the Gingers today. Mary Ann had brains and inner strength that put her on an equal footing in a man's world. She could be anything she wanted, but she also had a little Daisy Mae in her. Ginger had one thing working for her, and how long was that going to last?

I've noticed that young people go out and socialize in groups. Maybe that's their way of getting around the dating rituals. I think this is wonderful, up to a point. You get to know each other and you can size people up and still protect your feelings.

It's hard to imagine a Ginger fitting into a group, while a Mary Ann would be the glue that holds the group together. (By the way, I don't think the Gingers have a clue about the amount of genuine attention the Mary Anns get.) However, when you discover you have feelings for another and you find things in common, well, it is no longer group time. There is something special about being at a table, just the two of you. It's revealing. It's where the rituals become fun. It's not like every date has to create a deep moment, but where does it get you to remain intentionally shallow?

Mary Ann's lessons learned over time:

You should have male friends.
I do. They should be Big Brain friends. If he is married, his wife should know everything you do together.

Beware "The Road."
Men who travel for a living are capable of leading multiple lives.

Each new port can make his little brain feel like a New Man. Then, the New Man wants a new port.

Beware jealousy.
I don't trust men who are jealous. It's his little brain in overdrive. I think men who cheat are the most jealous.

Never tease.
If you tease, it means you aren't confident enough to appeal to a man's Big Brain. It's just bad manners.

Successful men attract women.
They just do. They light up your little brain and you must be careful. If you change your behavior — if you toss aside the Mary Ann in you — in the face of wealth and power, you will regret it.

Men who "play games" are just, well, awful.
Avoid them. I don't know which brain they think they are using. I think this is the kind of thing you do if you know, deep down, that you aren't interesting, so you manufacture these little dramas that make the days go by.

If it's all games, nobody wins.
If it's all about shallow things — what you wear, how you look and, especially, who wins the moment — it never gets deeper. My, what a waste of time — at least mine.

Half the world is populated by men.
Why on earth would you pursue a married one? If you have an affair with a married man you will be found out. It is impossible to keep it a secret. If he cheated on her, he will cheat on you.

Sooner or later, people want exclusivity.
You want to know you're the one. I've always been a one-man woman. It's deeper. It means something. If you don't have it, you're missing that something. Every man I've ever loved or cared about has been a best friend. No games. Person to person.

If someone truly wants to get to know you, they will.
Is this person concerned about me? Am I considered a real friend, a buddy? Are my thoughts and problems important? Do we share our selves equally?

Note to men — know this:
How you treat your daughter is how she will expect a man to treat her. If you are polite and kind and thoughtful, she'll expect it. If you're the opposite, that's what she'll expect.

You have to learn how to be a good mate.
To make it work you need to be part of a team, a good partner, even when you aren't together. That, in fact, may be the most important time.

If you have that nagging feeling that you missed one along the way . . .
You did.

Desire for money is not *desire*.
A woman who marries for money earns it every day.

Some men want only Gingers.
Let them go.

If all women were cherished and all men adored . . .
Oh, what a world this could be.

A personal note to the men in my life:

*The men and my life have been many — my father, my adopted brother, my cousins, nephews, godchildren, mentors, teachers, competitors, co-stars, business partners, special needs friends, fans, a husband, and couple of romances. All have made my life richer and you provided a great influence on how I perceive, treat, and react to the male species. I thank you. Like I said, **I love men.***

MARY ANN'S TERRIBLE TOO'S

Too protective

Too demanding

Too possessive

Too jealous

Too weak

Too cocky

Too fickle

Too insensitive

Too uncommunicative

Too egotistical

Illustration by James Bennett

A MAN'S MAN WITH DEPTH

Before Russell Johnson became the ever-steady Professor on *Gilligan's Island*, he usually played heavies and bad guys. He was a man's man who flew 44 combat missions in World War II, getting shot down once and earning a Purple Heart in the process .

He was handsome and smart. He had the funniest sense of humor of any of the cast. Along with humor, he brought tranquility to the cast. He was easy, a stable force with a twinkle in his eye. The man was never disagreeable.

Once when we were doing an appearance at Folsom Prison, Russell had to keep coming between me and a Hollywood star — who will remain nameless — who decided to develop an instant case of the hots for me. It all got as crude as Hollywood can get. Russell looked out for me well that day.

When I walked out on stage, the prisoners went berserk. When Russell walked out on stage, some guy yelled "I'll take him!" Russell said to me, "Now, it's your turn to get me out of here."

He lost a wife to cancer and a son to AIDS. He responded to both with a depth of character that could only come across in real life. He married one of his dear friends. Now that he is gone, his essence will always be a part of me.

civility

et • i • quette
noun

: the conduct or procedure
required by good breeding or
prescribed by authority to be
observed in social or official life

ELEGANCE

DECORUM

demeanor

courtesy

MANNERS

DIGNITY

propriety

Please pass the manners
Notes on courtesy, civility, grace . . . and booze

Manners are a sensitive awareness of the feelings of others. If you have that awareness, you have good manners, no matter what fork you use.

— Emily Post

There are more than 20,000 words in the English language. Seven of them are considered foul. You'd think somebody could write a screenplay and avoid The Seven. Is it that too much of an inconvenience? Apparently so.

Humphrey Bogart is on anybody's list of all-time great actors. His movies have withstood the test of time. Some are classics. Every single one of them would get a G-rating in today's Hollywood. Not one of them could be made and marketed today.

So, here we are. The idea of a common civility seems so lost. It's odd, because we know civilized behavior is classic, like Bogart. It's more odd because manners are easy to use and they cost nothing.

Look around. It's all casual. Casual conversation. Casual behavior. Casual Friday! Oh, the fine line between casual and sloppy.

Story time! When I first arrived in Hollywood I was invited to a dinner party. I was the guest of a CBS executive. One of the guests at the table was Jonathan Winters, at the time one of Hollywood's funniest comics and actors. To my surprise, he was a gracious gentleman. Sure, he knew which fork was which, but that hardly mattered. He never made the night about himself.

He took pains to include me in the conversation. He listened when I spoke. He was far and away the most intelligent conversationalist there. He cared about me. I was young. I was new in Hollywood and as green as I was, he acted as though my opinions were worthwhile. He was the essence of a gentleman. What a life lesson. He shared his humanity in a civilized way.

That's about all there is to it, really. Empathy, kindness, sensitivity, generosity, discipline, appreciation. These are all things that grow from courtesy. No, that's not quite right. You can't have these wonderful personal traits and not have manners. Manners are as much about knowing what to do as knowing how to do. It shows.

Jonathon Winters, one of Hollywood's finest comedians, made all the other men at the table seem like cardboard cutouts.

"Lady" and "Gentleman" are not bad words.

No, these words are not two of The Seven. Trouble is, you don't hear them enough. It's not about silk stockings and lifted pinkies. It's about being selfless.

Yes, that is manners, too. It isn't just the right fork. It isn't a bow and curtsy. It's civility. It is the opposite of your little brain. All you have to do is observe yourself. Which is your best foot and is it forward? When was the last time you sent an RSVP . . . on time?

Yes, there are rules and they can seem daunting if you are new to them. Some pretty hefty books have been written on the topic of manners. The basics, though, are pretty simple. I'll start with what I think is the single most important thing you can do to get on the Road to Being a Lady…thank you notes.

Yep. Thank you notes. It isn't the salad fork or the butter plate or the champagne flute or not texting at the table. These have their place and should be observed. Thank you notes, though, establish your Lady foundation. They also never hurt you.

Story time! I was once in the Detroit airport. I was to fly Delta Airlines to Los Angeles via Salt Lake City. I was very ill with a sinus infection.

A woman at the Delta counter told me I could fly non-stop to Los Angeles on a different airline — Northwest. I was so grateful. All I wanted to do was get in bed and get well.

When I arrived at Northwest I had no seat assignment. The woman at the Northwest counter was rude. After several attempts to get her attention she finally just refused to serve me. She was just awful and to this day I do not know why. Hey, I travel a lot. I know how stressful the jobs of airline personnel can be. I know how to get on a plane.

I finally gave up on her, found another attendant, went to another counter, and got the seat assignment in no time. I fumed all the way home, mostly because I never knew why she was so rude. I sent Northwest a complaint letter. They sent back two drink tickets for my next flight. It was about that time I began to feel guilty.

Two weeks prior to that incident I was booked on a Horizon Airlines flight from Boise, Idaho. I was on my way to host a conference in Oregon.

When I arrived at the airport, the women at the Horizon counter informed me that the flight was delayed because of weather. They couldn't have been nicer or more accommodating. They helped me book a room and they stored my luggage at the airport.

I thought, well, if I am going to write a letter of complaint to one airline, I should also write a thank you note to this airline. And I did. I received from Horizon a thank you note in reply. Now, I had never received a thank you note for a thank you note.

One thing led to another, and soon I was on the phone having a delightful conversation with an executive at Horizon. During that conversation I asked if the airline supported non-profits. They do. He directed me to the right people. I ended up with fifteen round-trip tickets that I was able to give to faculty and filmmakers at my Film Actors Boot Camp that year. What a delightful thing. Nice breeds nice.

I don't like the act of writing thank you notes. I only like having written them. It's one of those things that is just hard for me to do.

You have to find the time and then you have to find the words. So, I force myself. I leave the stationery and the envelope out on the desk. There it is, waiting, piling guilt on me every time I walk past until it gets written and, just like that, I feel like a better person.

I think my generation still works.

Socially, my generation offers — note I didn't say "offered" — a method of behaving. Let's call them The Rituals. The Rituals are a package deal of expectations.

When it's between a man and a woman, The Rituals are essential! They are there because men and women are different. We all know I'm capable of opening a door myself. I don't need to prove I'm strong enough to do it. The gesture means something else. It means, "I honor you." Understand the gesture and you separate yourself from the clueless crowd. (And ladies, if you do the inviting, you pick up the tab.)

The Rituals engage your Big Brain. The Rituals acknowledge that you are on the Road to Special. Without The Rituals you are on your own.

I was walking with a young man, much younger than me. I asked him if I could take his arm. Then I asked him to walk next to me on the side that faced the street. He wondered why. I explained that it is a gesture that comes from horse and buggy days. The streets were, well, less clean than they are today. There was stuff on the street you did not want on you, if you get my drift. The man is supposed to walk on the woman's street side in case a passing horse or buggy splashed some of the nasty stuff. He was there to block it. Today, "it" is splashes from passing cars.

This little educational moment absolutely delighted the young man. He took my arm. He placed himself on the street side. We started walking. No. He wasn't walking. He was *strutting*.

If you were never taught manners, it's not your fault. If you never learned manners, it is your fault. At first it seems like there is much to learn. It isn't just table manners.

There is business etiquette, hosting etiquette, interview etiquette, travel etiquette, phone etiquette, pet etiquette, disability etiquette, tipping etiquette, wedding etiquette…I think I'll stop there. I could go on.

Story time! I knew a young man who moved to Las Vegas while he was in his early twenties. He was a math teacher. He had little money, but he figured that Vegas would grow (he was right) and that he could create a new career there (right again).

The first thing he did on arrival was get a job at the best clothing store in town. He learned there how to dress like a gentleman (Cary Grant advised him to wear light colored socks).

He took courses in etiquette. He took dance lessons. He remade himself into a master of The Rituals, and in so doing, he created opportunities that led to his later success.

Get the basics down and learn the others when you need them. There isn't much point in boning up on wedding etiquette if you aren't going to one. When that day comes, get busy then.

When you do learn them, you will discover they are all variations of the basics. They are just applied differently in different situations. So, for your convenience, I have boiled down The Rituals to Mary Ann's Do's and Don'ts.

The Mary Ann Do's:

Use the magic words.
This is usually the first lesson we are taught as children. "Please" and "Thank you." They seem to be on the way out, replaced with casual versions intended to say similar things. There is no point in modernizing these expressions.

They say it all succinctly, meaningfully and without need of translation. On the other hand, "no problem" (what was the problem?) "no worries" (what are we worried about?) "I'm good," (have you been bad?) "have a good one," (a good what?).

Send thank you notes.
I know, I already covered this, so this is an opportunity for me to say it again. Write it by hand. Mean what you say. Get it in the mail on time. Within 24 hours.

Introduce people . . . and yourself.
Pet peeve here. Somebody comes up to me and says, "You don't remember me, do you?" Okay, now what? Do I fake it? Am I honest? Do I talk around it until the moment passes?

I've had this happen to me way too many times. I've waltzed around the conversation for ever so long, until it's over and *still* I never got a name. Erghh!

Introducing yourself is an art form. Here are some guidelines. You see someone you've met before. When you approach, there is that moment when you realize they don't recall your face or name. End the moment. Introduce yourself.

Sometimes the situation is reversed and you are the one who can't remember the face or name. There is that moment when you realize he remembers you. Prolong the moment — "Tell me again, where did we meet?" — until you extract an introduction.

You meet someone in unbalanced circumstances. You're busy. They're not. You're sober. They're not. You're distracted. They're not. The same can be said of them. That's why it's a mistake to assume people remember you. Introduce yourself. Get it out of the way.

Second pet peeve. Somebody walks up to me. She has a companion — a friend, a date, a spouse. It doesn't matter. She starts up a conversation and it goes into full swing. She brings the companion into the conversation. Meanwhile, you don't know who that person is. If you are escorting somebody, it is your responsibility to make the first introductions.

Hold the door.
This might also be entitled "Be Helpful." The idea extends way beyond a door, but this makes for a nice illustration. Make it a habit. Just do it all the time. The person coming through the door ahead of you or the one following you through the door doesn't have to be elderly or laden with packages. Just hold the thing open. It's nice. It says, "I respect you." It says, "You are important." Hold it for everybody. Old ladies. Little kids. UPS deliverers. What a nice habit to have.

Mind the table.
Consider table manners an act of survival. If you don't have them you will be left out in the cold. Worse, you won't know it. You

won't know what you missed or what opportunities passed you by because you lack table manners. Like it or not, table manners are an easy way for people to read you.

There is this notion that table manners are hard. Complicated! Yes, there is a difference between casual and formal manners, but not in spirit. Yes, there are more rules of etiquette associated with eating than most of the others. The basics aren't hard and I don't want to burden you with an entire chapter on them, but here's a starter: If your fork is in your fist and your chin is in your plate, maybe you want to look up some etiquette tips.

Keep your distance.
The modern term for this is "personal space." You want yours. Give others theirs. Here's the problem: People are, well, bigger now, to put it mildly. We live in a world where one thing we fear most is the middle seat on the plane. Squish. You are the one with no armrest or legroom.

Our private lives, our private selves, need boundaries. Just watch yourself. Are you standing too close? Are you poking his chest when you make a point? Do you bump into people on the side-walk without acknowledging them?

Do you give them room on the escalator? Worse, are you one of those people who get off the escalator and *stop and start looking around* while people are toppling behind you like lemmings? (Pet peeve for me. I travel so much. A girl could get hurt on an airport escalator.) It is a matter of being self-aware and thinking of others. Like all points of etiquette, it's a sign of respect.

Pay attention.

You're at a party. You're in a conversation. You start doing the "scalp stare" — your eyes search the rest of the room while the rest of you pretends to be fascinated. That never, ever works. If the most important thing that's going on at the moment is Who Else is Here, then go get a clipboard and take roll.

Here is a rule of thumb: *You know you are paying attention if you ask a question that takes the conversation deeper.* In other words, the conversation doesn't shift to you. If someone is discussing classical music and you instantly feel the need to list what you like or dislike, you aren't conversing. You're lecturing. Then again, if somebody *asks* you about classical music, let 'er rip.

Your phone.

Now, do I really need to stop at this point and tell you to put the phone down during a conversation? Maybe you come from the All Texts Are Urgent school. Ugh.

Sit up straight.

Maybe this one doesn't sound like etiquette to you. It is. Your body language speaks volumes. It talks about you and it says what you think. All manners are a form of respect. If you want to be draped in a chair or across a couch, go home. If you are with other people, you are not alone. Don't act like it.

Remove your hat.

This is an epidemic. A man's hat comes off indoors. Period. It is lifted in the presence of a lady. It is clean. Who cares, you say? I'm not a man. Okay. You see a couple in a restaurant. The guy has a stupid cap pulled down over his eyes. What does he look like?

The word "dolt" comes to mind. Let's say he's your guy. What do you look like? The woman with the dolt.

I love men, but they do need help from time to time. It's a simple gift you can give him. Make your demand known. Try to get the hat off. Ask gently with a smile. Still on? Ask again. Still on? Insist. Still on? Strike three, he's out.

If he puts it back on, well, maybe he doesn't want to be your guy that bad. If he's your husband and he puts it back on, well, time for a chat when we get home. Hey, even cowboys know how to remove a hat.

You should make your expectations known. If you want to be treated like a lady, demand it. If he just has to hide a bald spot, I don't know. Get him a beanie.

Story time! I was attending a party in southwest Virginia. Okay, it was my birthday party. A bluegrass group called The Southern Gentlemen played all day for us . . . and for me.

Along with being accomplished musicians, The Southern Gentlemen are all witty, gregarious, and well mannered. When they sang gospel songs, *they removed their cowboy hats.*

Know your place.
This is so misunderstood. It's a misreading of the idea of personal freedom. We live in a society like no other. We live surrounded by religious and cultural norms that may or may not make sense to you. If you pay attention, though, they will.

People aren't that different in their expectations. I mean, come on. Don't snap photos of yourself during a funeral. Use your Big Brain.

The Mary Ann Don'ts:

Don't be late.

There may not be a more revealing sign of disrespect than habitual lateness. It just screams "You don't matter. I do." Think of lateness as a tax your friends have to pay in order to be your friend. It's paid in minutes and frustration. Of course there are circumstances when lateness is forced upon you and those are understandable. Just don't be a habitual "tax collector."

Don't go first.

Going first is for children. This one goes along with Keep Your Distance and Know Your Place. Elevators. Food lines. Revolving doors. Any door. Going first is for people who can't control themselves. It's immature. It is the physical version of putting yourself first. When should you go first? When you are asked to.

We have now codified butting in line. As near as I can tell, this started in the late 1970s at a Manhattan nightclub called Studio 54. If you wanted to go in, you lined up. You gained entry only if the guys at the door approved you. It was arbitrary. Looks. Wealth. Fame. Whatever. It worked. The more they excluded, the more people sought inclusion. Go figure.

The Me First syndrome can grow on you if you aren't careful. It can be worse than your little brain is at work. It can be your dark side. It can make you see other people as lesser human beings. I have been, for example, in taxis and limos with celebrities who would abuse and berate the drivers until it made me cringe. In that situation, who, really, is the lesser human being?

Don't be noisy.
Another epidemic. You pay to see a movie and the woman sitting behind you talks through it. Her cell phone beeps. She answers it! "No, it's okay," she says, "I'm at a movie." Please tell me you aren't that person.

When you think about it, we have become movable noise generators. Sounds that did not exist not that long ago explode from our pockets and purses. Beeps and burps. Tinny jangles. Digital song bites. I don't know. So much has been said about cell phone abuse and it seems to have so little effect. Maybe just lower the volume.

If I had my way there would be phone booths again. Maybe those cute red English ones. There wouldn't be a phone inside. You could take your phone inside and chat away. I'd put them everywhere, inside and out. Hey, you want to live in a world isolated in your palm you might as well go to a nice quiet place and isolate yourself.

It doesn't have to be on the phone. I know people who Just Can't Stop Talking. During performances. During speeches. During prayers. During moments of silence! It just can't wait! In case you can't hear every word, they *can get louder* for you. Don't be that person. I don't think I've ever been told anything that couldn't have waited.

And then there are the Thumper Cars. You know the ones. The

car that vibrates with the sound from the stereo inside. The windows shake. Shoot, the *street* shakes. The car passes and you feel that you need a moment of recovery. It just has to hurt in there.

Don't honk.
I know this falls under Don't Be Noisy, but I want to carve out a special little place for this one. Is there such a thing as an intelligent honk? Answer: Yes. A honk is a warning. That's why it sounds the way it does. That's why it pierces the air and shouts down all other sounds. "Hey! Watch out!"

All other honks are, well, not intelligent. It's not designed to be an expression of anger or frustration or joy. It certainly isn't designed as greeting or an invitation. "Hey! I'm out here! On the curb! Get your butt in the car!" A honk is a one note song from a bad band with no lyrics.

Honks lead to bad things. It is the opening volley of road rage.

Don't correct.
This would be a good time to say that etiquette is *not* political correctness.

Etiquette comes to us honed by use. It has a long and worthy tradition of shared development. It is codified in books that are generally accepted as reliable. Political correctness is applied on the fly. It has a short history of top down, forced application. Whatever mandate it has lives in the minds of those who force it.

There is way too much not to like about political correctness for me to express it all here. Frankly, it surprises me how eager young people are to learn what the next thing they *can't* say is. People lose their careers over this stuff. Good people. Now, I wouldn't intentionally offend someone. Ever. I would never be deliberately rude. However it *isn't your business* to correct me if you think I have been politically incorrect.

Don't keep your seat.
Women get confused by this one. It's the man's role to stand when someone enters the room or approaches the table, right? Wrong. You should stand when you are approached by an elder. In crowded circumstances, you should give up your seat to an elder. Hey, *I'm* an elder. Let me tell you, the gesture is appreciated.

Don't show up uninvited.
Another epidemic. A text message that says, "Fantastic party now at Jolene's" isn't an invitation unless it comes from Jolene. Don't show up without notice. The same technology that allows the text message also allows you to deliver a heads up call, a little warning time. "I'm on Walnut Avenue. Okay if I drop by?"

Don't pick and scratch.
Ooh. We don't have that many orifices and we've only got ten fingers. Is it really that hard to keep them away from each other in public? Note to drivers: *We can see through your car windows.* It's not just bad manners. It's a turnoff.

Don't make out in public.
I have never understood this. I don't think you need to put a timer on a kiss. Actually, yes I do. Keep it short and preferably tongueless. Also, a booth in a bar isn't a private room.

Don't go shirtless.

This is a special bonus Don't. It is also a plea from me. America, please put your shirt on. Girls, you just have to explain to your men that back hair isn't an aphrodisiac. Cover up, for heaven's sake. Don't people have mirrors? Okay, if you've got that sculpted body with great abs, go find a beach or a gym. Thank you.

Special bonus manners hint!

Don't be in such a hurry. (Note to self: Listen to this one.) There is a song by the group Alabama, "I'm in a Hurry and Don't Know Why," which pretty much sums this up.

Here's the problem: Your little brain can convince you that what isn't urgent *is* urgent. It can be just another way of making it All About Me.

The pace of your life is controllable. Let your Big Brain control it. This will make you many things, including a better listener, which brings me to . . .

The art of conversation.

There is something special about a good conversationalist. These are people who engage and interest you. They build on what both of you are saying and enrich the conversation. A good lesson here might come from the Art of Improv.

Improvisation on stage requires one single method — never stop the flow. You are on stage. An actor rushes in. He says, "There is a dinosaur in the kitchen." If your response is "Dinosaurs are extinct," the improv is over. If you respond, "Where did you get such a big kitchen?" or "Is it one of those pink dinosaurs?" The improv stays alive and goes in directions unknown.

So, how does this apply to an offstage conversation? A real one? First you observe the Pay Attention rule in Mary Ann's Do's. After that, just keep in mind that what you are saying leads to something else, just like in improv. Let's start with the urge to relate your dislikes.

Conversationalist one: "My favorite part about Thanksgiving is the pumpkin pie."

Conversationalist two: "I hate pumpkin pie."

Done. Over. You can almost hear the thud. Here's another:

Conversationalist one: "I was stuck in traffic for hours. Every day it's like this. Why can't they fix it?"

Conversationalist two: "You think that's bad. I lost two hours waiting for a service call."

Yuck. Let's all get morose. Complaining is *not* conversation. Complaining is talking to yourself out loud. The two conversationalists we just read could probably go on for quite some time, expanding on their private complaints and never even acknowledging the other's.

Complaining, aside from being pointless, takes conversations in a downward direction. Complaints make conversations empty. I don't think I've ever *learned* anything from a complaint.

To me, the best conversations leave me knowing something new. That in itself is refreshing. It is uplifting. You can't learn anything talking about yourself.

People love to talk about themselves, though. As a good conversationalist, you can use this. We've all found ourselves in that awkward situation — you are in a group, maybe at a table and suddenly it all goes quiet. The air in the room just dries up. The voice inside your head is screaming, "Somebody say something!"

How do you restart the conversation? You introduce a topic that allows people to talk about themselves. I have a friend who uses a standard line in these situations. He'll say, "I read an article recently that said most people think they have handsome feet." Everybody, it seems, has an opinion about their own feet and they can't wait to chime in about it. The conversation is off and running again. Like improv, it goes in directions unknown.

Genuine conversation requires genuine participation. One of my traveling partners on a trip to Africa was a college president, a remarkable woman. I watched the world open up to her. How? She treated every person with respect. Even through the obstacle of translation, she engaged people. She listened. She shared. She learned. They were touched. People know when you genuinely respect them. You don't need a translator. It is a language all its own.

Is it possible to have a conversation without profanity? Yes. Do you have many conversations without profanity lately? I doubt it. I don't need to tell you that profanity is everywhere. There is no sanctuary. I am not immune to it.

IF YOU HAVE TO SWEAR, DO IT LIKE MR. MAGOO

Before Jim Backus was Thurston Howell III, he played many characters, but one stands out among them. Jim was the voice of Mr. Magoo, the bumbling, magnificently near-sighted cartoon character who refused to admit he had a vision problem. Like so many Backus characters, Magoo (first name: Quincy) was wealthy and easily annoyed by inconvenience. The result? A constant stream of mumbling from Magoo as he worked his way through each day. The mumbling was unintelligible, but Backus knew what he was saying. He gave voice to his own list of complaints. He told me, "If you ever see Mr. Magoo as he exits, I'm saying every dirty word you ever heard." I haven't seen the cartoon since he told me that, so I don't know if was telling me the truth or not (wink, wink).

Story time! I remember the first time I swore. I was a young adult. I was in my kitchen. I startled myself by saying the F-word. I stopped a moment and said it again. I started marching around the little butcher block table in the kitchen repeating the word at every step until I started laughing at myself and how ridiculous it sounds.

That was pretty much it. I haven't found much use for that or other swear words since. When I do, I am instantly ashamed of myself. I have to watch myself. I need to try harder. It is a habit that is easy to drift into. It can become second nature and meaningless.

I'm sure my mother never used a swear word. Wait! She did. At age 92 she smashed her finger with something, I don't recall what, and the S-word exploded from her mouth. We laughed about that one from that day forth.

In the right person, swearing becomes an art form — think drill sergeants and third base coaches here. It flows from them so naturally it doesn't even sound profane. You aren't an artist.

The opposite of swearing as an art form is the ubiquitous profanity we live with now.

It has no meaning.
It has no force.
It has no art.

We're desensitized. Vowing not to swear makes for a nice New Year's Resolution. Oh, how I wish more people would make it. (Note to self: this includes you. *What* would Mary Ann say?)

Booze.

The enemy of manners is alcohol. We all know this. Booze goes straight into your little brain. I think that's one of the reasons there is so much ceremony associated with drinking. The rites.

The flourishes. The protocols. The first sign that booze and your little brain are in control is when you start ignoring the ceremony.

I don't think booze ever affects the same two people in the same way. It depends on so many factors — how big you are, how tired you are, when you last ate, why you even want a drink — so many things.

It won't affect you the same way twice in a row. And let's face it, alcohol puts a different hold on different people. For some people, it's a light touch. For others it hangs on too long. For others it won't ever let go, like a trained Doberman.

Here's the problem. There is really only one way to learn about alcohol. Trial and error. Oh, the errors! You'd think that you could learn just by watching others. Oh, no. Booze and your little brain don't retain that kind of information. You will make errors. You have made them. The question is: How many times do you want to make the same error? I wish it were so easy to answer. Booze and your little brain don't even acknowledge errors. That's what your Big Brain gets to do tomorrow.

Story time! My father introduced me to alcohol. We had champagne at Christmas. I got to taste it. When I was 14 or 15, he took me to the liquor cabinet and gave me tastes of either scotch or bourbon. He used a spoon. Of course, it tasted dreadful to me. The point is, he took the mystery out of it. It really tasted awful. I don't think you can make a rational decision if alcohol is involved. You might think you are in charge of yourself. You might think you are making the right decision. It is your intention to do so.

Note: Your little brain is incapable of giving you a clear head. Your little brain tells you it's okay to drive. "I'm just buzzed." Your little brain is a follower. It gets its directions from somebody else's moral compass. The first thing your little brain tosses out is judgment.

How about if Mary Ann just offers a few suggestions? Consider these "pre-error" devices for young women, especially novices:

The name of the drink should also name the contents.
Gin and tonic. Bourbon and water. Scotch and soda. If somebody offers you a "Blue Motorcycle" or a "Singapore Sling" pass on it. These are drinks that combine different liquors that mask their obvious flavors. This usually creates a super strong drink with a Candyland taste. Don't go to Candyland.

The contents of the drink should be measurable.
A shot or a jigger of liquor is 1.5 ounces. One shot is a regular drink. Two shots is a "double." Don't drink doubles. The liquor portion of your drink should never exceed half the contents. Translation: 1 part bourbon to 1 part water is the max.

The strength of alcohol is measurable. Each bottle has a certain "proof" which informs you of its alcohol content. The higher the proof, the stronger the drink.

Of course, to follow this guideline, you need to watch the drink being made, or make it yourself, which is itself a pretty good idea. It won't take long, though, for you to judge the contents of your drink by look and taste.

Never drink the punch.
A frat house punch isn't a punch. It's Stupid Stew. Not only do you not know what's in it, you can't imagine what's in it.

Drink water.
This is a good way to slow down or clear your head. Let's say you arrive at a party in full swing. You get caught up in it. Fifteen minutes later you look in your hand to see your third drink. Call in the Big Brain! Put it down and drink a glass of water. You can pick drink number three back up later if you want. Club soda works, too, and it looks just like a drink.

Use math.
Beer and wine are measurable. Beer and wine name their contents. Beer and wine have predictable levels of alcohol. Call these the Math Drinks. If you can count you can pace yourself.

Make a drink diary.
This can be fun. Get some girls together at your place and make some drinks. Every half hour write down how much you've had and what you are feeling, or can't feel. Read it the next day and learn all the things your little brain wants to keep secret.

Drugs.

I don't even like to talk about drugs. Chances are you've never lived in a world free of drugs. Let me tell you, it was better. The choices just weren't there to be made. It was easier.

The landscape of drugs is changing and changing fast. Marijuana for medical use has been around for more than a decade. It is legal for recreational use in Colorado and Washington State as I write.

Look at me real hard as I write this. Most people, and this includes your friends, have *no idea* what they are talking about when they talk about drugs. I don't care how *expert* they sound.

Let's go back and look at Mary Ann's guidelines for alcohol. Can they be applied to drugs? Let's see these checkpoints:

Can you identify a drug's contents by its name?
Are the contents measurable?
Does the drug have a proof?
Do you know it's strength?
Can you make and measure it yourself?
Can you "use math" ?
Do you have any idea of "what is in the punch"?

If you answered "No" to these questions, and I'm guessing you did, then there really is only one conclusion: *You have to take the drug in order to find out what's in it.* What? Are you kidding me?

Would your Big Brain ever, ever, ever, *ever* (four evers!) do that, especially after you understand that one or two events with the wrong drug can ruin you? *Forever.*

In the end, it's censorship.

Censorship. It's become a bad word. (Funny, the word "ban" has never been more in vogue, but that's for another book.) Back to censorship. That, really, is what we've been talking about in this chapter, isn't it? Manners and etiquette are nothing more than self-censorship. Let's talk about it.

Story time! When we filmed *Gilligan's Island*, cleavage was measured in inches and seconds. Tina's cleavage could only be so deep and the camera could not linger there longer than about three seconds at a time.

The Mary Ann costume had to conceal my navel. The cameramen were supposed to monitor this during shooting. Sherwood Schwartz used to say that between my navel and Tina's bosom, he wore out the path from his office to the studio just answering cameraman calls.

The Howells had to have twin beds in their hut. They could never be in bed together with all their feet off the ground. There is more. A lot more. I won't read you the entire handbook (there was one). It all sounds so overdone today, doesn't it? Or does it?

Would a little censorship hurt today? I'd take it. What are we really talking about here? Is censorship oppression or is it an act of civic responsibility?

The cultural standard falls. The new lower standard becomes the norm. The lower standard falls. You are on your own.

You can be your own sanctuary.

I really need to make sure I'm not misunderstood here. I am not about to say that you should isolate yourself. You just need to understand who and where you are.

We are an urban people. This is new. More people live in cities now than live in rural areas. What does this mean? You have a lot more to bump into. You have much more coming at you. Meanwhile, things are getting more coarse as they get more crowded. You can either be swept up and carried along in this or you can be an island of civility.

If you walk down the street and smile, people will smile back. If you truly engage people in conversation, they will talk back. Kind words generate warm responses. If you write thank you notes, people will remember you. If you say "please" and "thank you" and "pardon me" and all the rest, you will never, ever be wrong.

On the other hand, if you look like you just came out of a police lineup, well, what do you expect? Behave as a lady and you'll find you can get almost anything you want.

Perhaps sanctuary is the wrong word. Maybe the word should be island. Maybe it should be should be your own *island*. When you think about it, *Gilligan's Island* was a wonderful place to be marooned.

The castaways treated each other with a sense of propriety and empathy. They took care of each other. There was a decorum. There was a sense of shared destiny.

No wonder the show is still welcomed into people's homes.

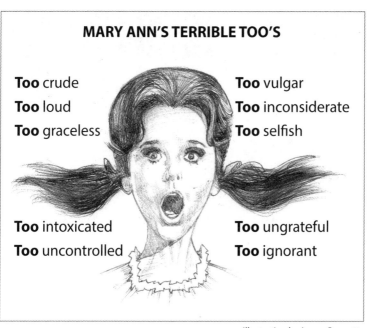

MARY ANN'S TERRIBLE TOO'S

Too crude   **Too** vulgar

Too loud   **Too** inconsiderate

Too graceless   **Too** selfish

Too intoxicated   **Too** ungrateful

Too uncontrolled   **Too** ignorant

Illustration by James Bennett

encouragement

confidence

HOPEFULLNESS

faith

op • ti • mism

noun

: a feeling or belief that good
things will happen in the future
: a feeling or belief that what you
hope for will happen

brightness

CHEER

I can't imagine a life without dancing
Optimism, the first cousin of perseverance

You'll never find a rainbow looking down.

—Charlie Chaplin

My father always said he named me Dawn because everything beautiful starts with a new day. I guess you could say I was made an optimist at birth.

When you think about it, there isn't much point in being anything else, is there? I think of myself as a natural optimist. Still, I think you have to work at it. Optimism doesn't seem to be a natural state for most people. Look at the news. Doom and Gloom sells. You'll never see a headline that says "299,999,999 Americans didn't commit a crime today."

We have to be told to count our blessings. Shoot, it's the name of a song (Bing Crosby, *White Christmas*). It's so easy to awaken to a day and see only the burdens. You might even dread them.

On *Gilligan's Island*, why didn't the castaways all just give up and kill each other? It was an optimistic show. The situations were resolved with humor. It was a reflection of its creator, Sherwood Schwartz, one of the few people I could describe as a total optimist in his writing.

He defied the odds and the critics and was determined to make the show work. He saw something good in it. When it was test marketed, it got the highest test market score CBS had ever seen. (I think that's true, but I don't have time to look it up.) Why didn't the critics get it? I don't know. They still don't get it. Luckily, a worldwide audience for the last fifty years did get it. The critics just do not understand this audience — which, by my count, is almost everybody. Maybe the critics don't understand optimists.

If you were cast in a role, what would it be?

Your optimism, or lack of it, shows. It is in your expression, your posture, your walk, your voice, your eyes. Imagine you are being sized up by a casting director. What would they see in you?

Now cast yourself in the scenes of your daily life — arising from bed, navigating traffic, at the coffee shop, at work. Now, watch yourself, become your own audience. What kind of story are you living out? Are you a creative force or are you sidetracked by money, time, relationships, work . . . life? As the lead actor in your own story, how would you review yourself? Does your story have enough heart in it? Are you showing the heart?

You know the phrase "Live on stage." Well, are you? Are you alive? Are you receptive to what is good in this world?

Nothing starts with the word "No." You can stop anything before you start. A friend of mine loves to ride his bicycle. Riding a bike is part of his daily life — short rides, long rides. He rides to the store. He rides to bars. He always says that before each ride, he considers canceling it. It is, after all, faster and easier in a car.

He lives on a hill. He knows that every ride starts with an easy coast and ends with a difficult climb. Does he want to make that climb? Again? That's really the question. His answer is always *yes*.

He wants to mix it up. He wants to get in the game. So what if it's a little gray and chilly out there? He suits up and spends a little time outside and it's not so bad. He warms up his legs on a climb and it's just another day on the bike. By the time he gets back home, it doesn't seem so gray and chilly at all. He doesn't even want to go back inside.

The point is, he didn't have to *force* himself to go out and get on that bike. Experience had taught him, time and again, that it would be worth it. He knows that when he confronts that hill at the end of his ride he will *want* to ride back up. He's optimistic. He cast himself into that role. Knowing you will accomplish something makes you look forward to it.

Get in the dance.

When I was young, my father would take me out on the dance floor. The orchestra at the Thunderbird Hotel would play dance music before the floor show started. He was a very big man. He taught me all the ballroom dances. He was fantastic dancer and very good at the Rumba. When a big man can do the Rumba with rhythm and subtlety, it is something wonderful to see. Not a showoff, but a good dancer with great rhythm.

I was about ten years old. I couldn't even see over his shoulder. Oh, how proud I was he wanted to dance with me!

I don't think you can dance and be unhappy at the same time. It's an expression of joy. It's humanity expressed by each generation, from the minuet to the jitter bug. Try it when you feel down. Put on your favorite dance rhythm and see what happens.

I think all men should learn to dance. It may sound old-fashioned. I'm not talking hip-hop. It's foxtrot, swing, waltz, rumba, cha-cha and just a touch of slow dance. To a Mary Ann, there is no difference between a waltz and a square dance. It isn't the steps. It's just a matter of the music she likes. She would stay on the dance floor. She would dance through life . . . and she *is*.

Optimism doesn't make you a Pollyanna. You don't have to look for Utopia. It isn't there. You are far better off observing the thousands of kindnesses and willing sacrifices that surround you every day. People behaving with good will toward other people. They are there!!! (*Three* exclamation points.)

People are more good than bad.
More nice than mean.
More positive than negative.

That's not the view of a hopeless romantic. It's the view from where I stand. And I have stood here for more than three generations.

Your state of affairs and your state of mind.

You couldn't find an aspirin in my grandmother's house. Her motto was "I'm not getting sick." She was older. She had her aches and pains, but she just moved them aside and kept going. She embraced what happened to her every day. That's optimism!!! . . . ! (I just *had* to add one more.)

She never complained and she never nursed bad feelings. If she and my grandfather had a disagreement, she went outside and picked flowers.

I was grateful to get that from her. I'm grateful to be here. I feel fortunate to have love and health and ambition and intelligence and discipline and curiosity. You can't get any of those from the store.

Optimism and pessimism multiply themselves, like those amoebas splitting in the petri dish.

I think having children makes people optimistic. Life begins anew. They see familiar things with new eyes. Each day is a new triumph. Look! She's growing! She's walking! A child can seem like a bouncing package of tomorrows.

I'm a debater. I always look at both sides. I think it's a wonderful way to look at life. It lets you see what is good and bad in perspective. When you get older, you figure out there is a cost to everything. Everything. You need the rain, but you also get the floods.

Debate makes me think, but sometimes I like the side of me that feels. I have these moments. I can picture one now. I am at my ranch. I'm in the backyard by the pasture. My horse is coming to me for his apple. At that moment of our communication, I feel small next to this magnificent animal. I am filled with joy. I could explode with happiness. His strength, his power, his affection, these become my necessities.

At the same time, I can have a similar moment with my little cat — a moment beyond the exchange of food or care — it is a soul and energy connecting.

I feel sorry for people who don't have these moments of connection and communication. It's important to feel! If you are only led by your head, you are missing something. More than something. You are missing yourself. You can have that moment at any age.

It's not what you see, but how you see it.

I don't trust people who don't like animals. Wait, that's not it. I don't *distrust* them — I just think there is something basic that is missing. I don't know why. It just doesn't seem right. The way people interact with pets tells me a lot about them.

Story time! A man who was a friend of mine for years was visiting me. My cat was on his lap. He said, "Dawn, there is something wrong with your cat."

Well, I wondered what that could be and we set about examining the cat. My friend kept referring to the abnormal sounds my cat was making. After a few minutes I realized what he meant. I looked at him and said, "That's the sound of purring."

I felt sorry for him. A grown man who never had an animal. It seems unusual. There is so much a child can learn about unconditional love and responsibility from an animal.

Meet the first cousin of perseverance.

I thought about what follows for a long time. It struck me that I could write all the uplifting words I could think of, or I could inspire you with a true story. It's the story of a man, the son of my dear friend, Gail. I called her. Could I put Jimmy's story in a book? "Yes."

This story is for you to keep in mind whenever things seem dark to you. When everything's at stake. It is the story of my dear friend, Jimmy.

Jimmy was a normal baby at birth. At twenty months he had a re-action to a routine shot. We know today that the odds of that re-action were one in three million. He suffered brain damage. Gail was told that Jimmy would probably not talk again and perhaps not ever walk. All the important skills that are learned during the first developmentally important twenty months were lost.

At age two, Jimmy began having seizures. At three, he was diagnosed with epilepsy. His coordination was poor. He speech was unintelligible. It was a moment of truth for Gail. What kind of future could he have? It was at this moment she put aside the warnings and predictions of experts. She took over.

She began by having him sing. Every day. She started with simple songs. She began by having him work puzzles. Every day. She started with simple puzzles. She had him climb trees. Every day. She started with simple trees.

As the songs and the puzzles and the trees grew, step by step, more complex, Jimmy's coordination and his confidence grew (and so did Gail's). By age five he was given roller skates. He had an odd skating style, shooting out his right leg and dragging his left.

And something happened.

Jimmy wasn't just a kid who could skate. He was a kid who could skate *faster* than the other kids. His confidence grew. He was up on one water ski by age nine. He swam. He hopped around on a Pogo stick for hours.

And something happened.

With adolescence came a new attack of seizures. He was medicated and, in turn, became slow and confused. More seizures. More medicine. More slowness. More confusion. He was hospitalized for months. After his release from the hospital, he was sent to special schools.

His short term memory was all but gone. Gail kept telling him it was "just one more mountain to climb."

One day, Jimmy asked his mother to go to lunch with him. He said, "These are my mountains, now." He wanted to go to high school. A *real* high school.

High school? He wouldn't even be able to remember where his locker was, much less find his classes. He won. He went to high school.

And something happened.

He joined the cross country track team and ended up being the first sophomore to ever be lettered. It was quite an accomplishment, which was not without its comical moments. Cross country means just that and all was great until he started to lead the pack and of course forgot where he was supposed to go. His sister and mother placed themselves along the route so they could yell "Turn here! Go *left* for goodness sakes! Just *go*!"

His track skills got him into college, where he was able to stick it out for a couple of years.

He went to work, but frustrated employers. How were they to deal with his lack of memory? He began cutting lawns and built up a clientele.

Here I need to say that the seizures and the side effects of medicine never went away during all this time. They grew worse. The combination of the medicine and the seizures made him appear, as he said, "stupid."

And something happened.

Jimmy decided he wanted a radical procedure. The damaged half of his brain would be removed so the seizures would stop. The risks were high — possible loss of speech and motor skills, inevitable pain and lengthy recovery time and expense. He wanted it. He fought for it. He got it.

The surgery was successful. During the procedure, it showed

that all this time, the right side of Jimmy's brain was doing all the work. The left side was all but gone.

Today Jimmy runs a successful retail shop. He is in charge of it. It is his. The decisions are his. He is independent.

Every point in Jimmy's story where "something happened" was preceded by a decision to take control. It was one thing to "not give up." That's perseverance. It is another to find a new way. That's optimism.

In so many ways, this is the story of Jimmy's mother, Gail, too. Without the singing and puzzles and tree climbing, there never would have been the skates. Without the skates there never would have been the confidence. Without the confidence, there never would have been the whole Jimmy we have today.

So, what are Mary Ann's thoughts on optimism?

Your little brain and your Big Brain are both optimists.
There's a difference. One is a wishing brain. The other is a working brain.

Your little brain sees through rose-colored glasses.
Your Big Brain looks for a clear space in your windshield.

Optimism lights the way on the Road to Special.
And it tells you to stay on the Road.

Optimism tells you it's worth the trip.
Pessimism tells you that your brakes might fail. You have to work

My dear friend Gail and my hero, Jimmy. His sister, Cynthia, is my heroine.
Cynthia is totally deaf and is raising two wonderful children with the help of
LaRue, her hearing dog. Photo: Dawn Wells Archives

at keeping pessimism away. It's too easy to see roadblocks. It's too easy to defeat yourself on the way. It's too easy to pull off the Road to Special. Optimism keeps you going.

Optimism is always forward looking.
Optimism tells you that you will clear the hurdle the next time you vault.

Optimism defuses arguments.
It points people in the same direction. It illustrates that we are more alike than we are different.

Optimistic people are healthier.
At least, they look that way to me.

Optimists aren't afraid of the truth.
Optimists ask the real questions. Optimists understand risks.

MARY ANN'S
TERRIBLE TOO'S

Too bleak

Too morbid

Too fatalistic

Too gloomy

Too cynical

Too scornful

Too spiritless

Too forlorn

Too cheerless

Too negative

Illustration by James Bennett

HE NEVER MET A STRANGER

Every time Alan Hale hugged me, my feet left the ground. He was a big man in every way. The man was never, ever cranky.

He grew up in a Hollywood family. His father played Little John in the classic Errol Flynn version of *Robin Hood*.

His mother was a silent film actress. So Alan grew up with his heroes — Flynn, Roy Rogers — in his home. He loved playing the role of the captain. He had a long career and made hundreds of TV and film appearances.

I understand that when he heard of the *Gilligan's Island* part, Alan was making a Western in Utah. He rode his horse to the highway and hitched into Los Angeles for the audition.

What you saw on film was what you saw in person. He could fill a room with his smile. A great guy. He was everybody's friend. So full of laughter and gentleness for his size. I never saw him angry or disgruntled. I think he was permanently gruntled (is that a word?). He had no trace of a star's ego.

Nothing more special than a hug from Alan. Photo: Dawn Wells Archives

recognition

fame

noun

: the condition of being known
or recognized by many people
a: public estimation : reputation
b: popular acclaim: renown
archaic: rumor

IMMORTALITY

ESTEEM

STARDOM

eminence

glory

acclaim

Notice me!
Notice me!
Notice me!
False fame and its evil twin – gossip

*I always want to say to people who want to be rich and famous —
"try being rich first." See if that doesn't cover most of it. There's not
much downside to being rich, other than paying taxes and having
your relatives ask you for money. But when you become famous,
you end up with a 24-hour job.*

— Bill Murray

Just before the turn of the twentieth century, a young man named
L. Frank Baum — who would later in life pen the classic *The
Wizard of Oz* — set out for a life in theater. However, he had
a problem. Baum came from a prominent, well-to-do family
and his chosen profession — the theater — was considered . . .
hmmm, well, unsavory.

In the eyes of many . . . No! In the eyes of most, theater people
were little better than con men, hustlers, and ladies of the night.
To avoid shaming his family, Baum wrote and performed in those
days under an assumed name.

By the time I arrived in Hollywood fifty years later, the entertainment world had evolved into a mature and popular industry. The
shame was replaced by fame. The full power of the reach of tele-

vision was just beginning to emerge. The entire idea of syndicated reruns that could perpetuate a television persona was unknown.

I had no idea what ratings meant. I only dimly understood fame. I had no idea that I could, and would, remain Mary Ann for the next fifty years.

Today, fifty years after *Gilligan's Island* first lit up television screens in black and white, I am stunned to see what people will do to get themselves on television. Mostly, I'm talking reality TV here.

People will crawl through slime — literally! — to be on screen. It seems the road to television time is paved with endless humiliations. I've seen people eat bugs! All this for a moment of fame. Fifty years ago it was seven castaways making their world the best it could be for each other on a deserted island. Today, the question is who will get thrown *off* the island. Hmmm. Maybe we've come full circle from L. Frank Baum's day.

If it isn't television, it's a parallel digital life on social media. Do you really want to put every waking moment up as a new post on the internet? For strangers? You want everybody to know…what?

Okay, pause button. I know it is easy for people who have enjoyed fame to pooh-pooh it. I'm not doing that. I have seen both sides of fame. There was a time when I couldn't walk through an airport unnoticed. Well, now sometimes I can, and I like it.

You hear celebrities say "Be careful what you wish for." They say that for a reason. To be a young Dawn Wells at the height of fame today would drive me nuts. This is, after all, the age of cell phone cameras, Google Glass and YouTube, TMZ, and *The Enquirer*. Trust me, you don't want to be fodder for these people. I don't need to tell you that it is usually the stories of your blunders that go viral, true or false.

I prefer the Dawn of today. I'm in charge of my own little world. What fame I have has been a blessing to me. I hope that I have used it well. The point is that fame does not consume my whole life. If I am going to be noticed, I want to be noticed for a good reason.

The wrong people are famous today. Fact. A *sorry* fact. It wasn't that long ago that heart surgeons, explorers, test pilots, inventors, architects — people who accomplished things — were celebrated. They were on the magazine covers.

When Jonas Salk developed the first polio vaccine in the mid 1950s, the vaccine became known worldwide as the Salk Vaccine. When Robert Jarvik installed the first artificial heart in the early 1980s, he became a household name. It became The Jarvik Heart.

Today, it seems that the people who *pretend* to be heart surgeons, explorers, test pilots, inventors and architects are celebrated. I'm talking actors, here. Throw in athletes and there you have it, the pantheon of fame. Wait, we need to include another category: People Who Are Just on Television . . . Because. This is a separate category that takes us into the Famous for Being Famous category, which takes us into . . . oh, nevermind. They really aren't worth the ink.

Break out your old clipboard and go interview twenty people on the street. Ask them to name the judges on the Supreme Court. Then ask them to name the judges any of those television talent shows. Want to bet which set gets the most correct answers?

I recall a friend who described celebrities as lab rats. Here was his theory: We give a person everything on earth we think people really desire — fabulous wealth and extravagance. The best of everything! Front row tickets to life! Then, we watch to see what they do with it, especially when they self destruct on too much of a good thing.

Here's the point: Fame comes and goes. Accomplishment sticks around. Fame without accomplishment is empty. With that in mind, here are . . .

Mary Ann's Life Lessons About the Desire for Fame:

Know your goal.
If your goal is to be adored, well, good luck. That isn't a goal. *It's a longing too deep for tears.* It is what your little brain wants. The applause! The crowds! The ecstasy! Most people have no idea how much work goes into keeping celebrities in the public eye. Those celebrity shows. Those paparazzi shots. The trash mags. Those "shocking revelations."

Oh, how they rise to the top, fall to the bottom and then "find new inner peace." Do you really think that's journalism? If Being Famous for Being Famous is your goal, be prepared to work for it. You'll end up working harder than you would if you actually accomplished something worthy of fame.

NOW *THIS* IS TABLOID MATERIAL

Years ago I was hiking with my friends Marcia and Jim in a region above Mammoth Lakes in California. It was a carefree, silly day. I recall we hiked and sang "Hi Ho, Hi Ho" like the Disney seven dwarfs.

We ended up three miles deep in the forest alongside a beautiful river. The river was wide and dotted with big rocks. We loved the spot. It seemed like it was the middle of nowhere. Marcia and I turned to Jim and said, "Jim, you hike that way for about a mile. Marcia and I are going to skinny dip." Off he went.

We stripped and swam and then we sunbathed nude beside the river. It was a drowsy, sunny afternoon and we were lulled into sleep. Lulled, that is, until we heard giggles and chatter from the other side of the river. It was a cub scout troop . . . and their leaders.

I turned to Marcia and said, "Let's just take it slow and casually get dressed because I don't think any of these boys have ever seen a naked woman before, other than maybe their mother."

We rose slowly and began to dress like it was a normal moment. I just about had all my clothes on when Marcia screams, "Guess who this is! It's Mary Ann from *Gilligan's Island*!"

To this day, I wonder if the scoutmasters used their binoculars. At least they had a story to tell. And thank heaven, it was before cell phones with cameras. Whew.

Do the work first.
If you do something well, you may or you may not become well known. If you do something better than anybody else, you will become well-known. Either way, you have to do the work. Fame isn't the answer. Doing the job is the answer. The joy is in the process. The years I spent making 98 episodes of *Gilligan's Island* were some of the happiest and most fulfilling years I've had. It didn't seem like work, but it was. It's odd, in a way. The show itself made the cast well-known. The re-runs made us famous. The work we put into the show was the gift that kept on giving.

Use your prestige.
Being known, being prominent, gives you influence. You are listened to. Hollywood stars are forever being asked to lend their names to causes and charities. Eventually, they usually just pick one that has great personal appeal for them. You don't have to be a global phenomenon to make this work for you. You can be a successful high school coach and be a force for good in your community.

Don't abuse your prestige.
This is absolutely the worst. It's when confidence morphs into false pride. If you ever find yourself asking someone this question, "Do you know who you are talking to?" go and wash your mouth out with . . . something. I've seen this too often. It's when you start thinking of yourself as special and everyone else as "The Other."

Be prepared for the worst.
Do you really want your life to be an open book? Well, if we use social media as a model, apparently so. Well, reconsider. It's not

all applause and camera flashes. Understand that with fame, privacy becomes a luxury. You don't know what the butler is telling people. One leak — true or untrue — and you can get paranoid. Information about you becomes valuable. It can be sold.

Story time! A few years ago, I was sitting in a small restaurant at a private party and talking with Connie Stevens. We had just appeared in a small film festival. We were having one of those "Oh, my! The state of things today!" conversations. I think we mentioned the aggravations of selling some properties we both had in Idaho and Wyoming. Smalltalk. A few days pass and I read in the gossip press that I'm broke and homeless and an addict.

The news goes viral. *Mary Ann in the dumpster!* It was out and I couldn't stop it. Totally untrue, of course. What? Not again. No truth to it. In this case the price of fame is filling somebody else's pocket. I don't understand how people can get paid — and actually accept the money — at the expense of someone else *when it isn't true and they all know it.*

Which brings me to . . .

Gossip.

Gossip is an industry. That we know. Gossip appeals to our lesser angels. That we know, too. Gossip makes weak people think they are popular. "Cluster around me! I've got some dish!"

I think inside information has grown way out of proportion in show business. In the entertainment world, we are almost ruled by gossip. It has become news. Shoot, there is an entire TV channel devoted to it. I never conceived that I would be this concerned about my private life at this age.

I think it goes back to the "Too many Gingers" phenomenon. It's surface. It's shallow. It's making unimportant things seem important. And so, in response . . .

Mary Ann's Life Lessons About Gossip:

What makes a person interesting?
Here's the rule of thumb:

Interesting people talk about *ideas*.
Average people talk about *things*.
Dull people talk about *other people*.

In other words, gossip is the voice of your little brain. I've never known this not to be true.

If someone gossips with you, they will gossip about you.
Think about it. How can it be "just among friends" if it isn't friendly? A gossip is a gossip. A gossip is not to be trusted. A gossip is not a good person, certainly not a good girl. A gossip is a walking little brain.

Avoid them. Shut them off. Watch a gossip's response when you say, "I don't need to hear about that. Why do we need to talk about it?" Try it. The gossip will look like you just told her the Earth isn't round. You won't lose a friend. A gossip can't be a genuine friend. You might actually awaken a gossip's Big Brain. Bravo!

It is better to be gossiped about than to be a gossip.
The only upside about being the target of gossip is that it means you are the interesting one. At least you are more interesting than the gossips. As a practical matter, there is nothing you can do about gossip, true or untrue.

Be careful if you get the urge to return fire.
That's your little brain at work. Oops! Suddenly you are at the same level. Shame on you! The best you can do is go on being you. Hey, when the worst gossip about me hit the media, it ended up being a bonus. I got a bunch of time on air. "Look! The Shocking Revelation!" Mary Ann is . . . quite normal.

Good girls don't do it.
No, they don't. It isn't classy. It's destructive. What if it isn't true? What if it is? When it's "just among friends" there is a huge difference between exchanging gossip and expressing concern.

Good girls are concerned. If Suzy Q doesn't seem like herself lately, maybe it's time for her friends to put their heads together. If you saw Suzy Q make a fool out of herself last night, maybe it's time to keep that to yourself.

If you hear gossip about a friend, do you inform her? Hmmm. What then? You have to be prepared to answer the question, "Who told you that?" Suddenly you are an unwilling rider on the Trash Talk Merry Go Round.

Are you a gossip?
Simple test here. If someone tells you something gossipy, do you repeat it? How many times do you repeat it? Ever ask yourself

why? Can you be trusted with a secret? Truth now. Can you? If your friend got an awful haircut, do you honestly tell her, or cruelly tell others? Think hard about this. Be honest.

Do you see successful people and want to knock them off their pedestals? Are you more interested in people's imperfections than their accomplishments? Does it make you feel better? I can't imagine a daily routine, a daily pastime, that depends upon *what other people do.*

I want you to be known for your accomplishments.

I want you to be comfortable with yourself. I want you to like yourself for who you are. I want you to make who you are even better. Get on the Road to Special. Here is a certainty: False fame doesn't move you down the Road to Special. Making others seem less special actually takes you off the Road to Special.

I spent some time considering how I should wrap up this chapter. I decided to quote this sobering stanza from the classic poem, "Elegy Written in a Country Churchyard" by Thomas Gray. It was published in 1751.

The boast of heraldry, the pomp of power,
And all that beauty, all that wealth e'er gave,
Awaits alike the inevitable hour.
The paths of glory lead but to the grave.

MARY ANN'S TERRIBLE TOO'S

Too scandal mongering
Too much of a busybody
Too exaggerated
Too conspicuous
Too affected
Too critical
Too flaunting
Too meddling
Too gossipy
Too snoopy

Illustration by James Bennett

A CELEBRITY WHO DIDN'T WANT CELEBRITY

Bobby Denver was very special and people never saw the many sides of him. He was very deep and very smart. He didn't share himself easily.

He became the characters he played. I think that's why viewers loved him. He was the essence of his characters. He wasn't an "actor." He *was* Gilligan. He *was* Maynard. He *was* every character he played. He was very, very private.

He wasn't particularly funny in person. He was intellectual and shy. Somehow, Bobby and I connected.

His last marriage to Dreama was wonderful. He had several children. He was wonderful with all children. His last son was a special needs boy. Bobby often communicated to me how blessed he was to have Colin and that they shared a special relationship.

The solemn, introspective, gentle, "real" Bobby. Photo: Dawn Wells Archives

Bob and Dreama, two of my best friends. Photo: Dawn Wells Archives

His lifestyle was unusual and "organic" before anyone ever heard the word.

Kids would follow him like he was a Pied Piper. One day he showed up on the set with dark circles under his eyes. He had stayed up all night making a spider farm with his kids. He *had* to name all the spiders.

He was a celebrity who didn't care for celebrity. I think he was comic genius.

attraction

beau•ty

noun

: the quality of being physically attractive
: the qualities in a person that give pleasure to the senses or the mind
: a beautiful woman

grace

Allure

glamor

CHARM

The allure of being alluring

Beauty, fashion,style . . . and that $500 purse

A girl should be two things. Classy and fabulous.

— Coco Chanel

When I say "You are on your own" in this chapter, it's a good thing. It's a great thing. How's this? You have never been more free to make yourself look good. The Fashion Gods that women once served now serve us.

We are not at the mercy of hemline dictators. We can pick and choose. We can be ourselves.

Take a look at photographs from the last 40 years. You can easily identify the time period of photos taken in the sixties, seventies and eighties just by looking at the clothes and hairstyles. (A question to the Fashion Gods: Did you enjoy that vacation from reality you took during the Sixties and Seventies?)

The Eighties! Oh, my heavens, those shoulder pads! (Along with the high hair, they *did* slim my hips.) A look of feminine power!

It gets a little harder in the nineties. Today, there is no conforming look.

The question is, what are you doing with all this freedom? Oh, dear! Honey, you are going to need your Big Brain.

Dawn isn't here to tell you what to wear, that spectator pumps and a string of pearls are always in style (they are), that if you are small you shouldn't wear huge collars (you shouldn't) or that a combo of Daisy Dukes, high heels and a halter is a bad interview look for any business that doesn't have barstools (it is).

I'm here to explain that style and beauty are inseparable from you. The real you, not a manufactured you. Not a storebought you.

So, with that in mind, here are Mary Ann's Style Points:

Know what colors look good on you.
. . . and which ones do not! If you have to have a certain dress whose color doesn't work well with your skin tones, adjust your make-up base or accessorize with a scarf around your neck that complements the dress but also complements your skin tones. Buy with your color in mind.

Understand your body shape.
There are certain styles that can complement any body shape while others can point out uncomplimentary aspects of the physical you. For example, if you have big hips, you don't want to wear a dress with a gather or a peplum or ruffles on the hips. Camouflage your flaws. Emphasize your assets!

Know when to use make-up.
. . . and how to apply! You can go to a makeup counter in almost

any department store and get a free consultation. If you really know what you are doing, this is helpful. If you don't, be cautious. You know your face better than anyone.

You know the colors that look better on you than anyone. You aren't getting a commission for the sale. Yes, they will try to sell you their products, too. But hey, you might need them.

Here are some rules I follow:

- Makeup should be subtle. It's highlights and shadows.
- Know your palette. Are you warm or cool?
- Use a magnifying mirror, at least 5X in strength.
- Apply makeup in daylight if possible, in bright light if not.
- Take a photo of yourself after your makeup is on. Save it.
- Review yourself in a mirror in daylight.
- False eyelashes are great. Learn how to wear them.
- Don't confuse daytime makeup and glam makeup.
- Your eyes and your mouth are your assets.
- You can keep up with a trend, but keep it subtle.
- Never sleep in your makeup. It's bad for your skin.

Glam highlights and sparkles, lip gloss, extra blush, and thicker lashes are for evenings or special events. So, glam it up!

My routine: I think of it as a checklist a pilot checks off before he takes off. I give myself an hour for hair and makeup. I wash my face.

Until the last few years I used a medicated makeup underneath everything to dry my skin. I no longer need that.

If you use moisturizer, apply it first. I don't use it. I use Erase to highlight or cover any imperfections, then I use a liquid base with a moistened natural sponge. It is applied very lightly.

Next step, use the same sponge for pancake makeup. I use MAC. My color is dark oriental (I have *no* pink in my skin). Then I powder with a light, loose powder — the whole face. I then contour with blush and shadow.

I then do my eyes. Here I need to stop and say that everybody's eyes are different. This is a good place to experiment. The same goes for lip colors.

I always always always (*three* always!) remove my makeup before I go to sleep. I remove it all with Albolene and then wash with soap and water.

Never forget that makeup is an illusion. It is the subtle emphasis of highlights and shadows. It is not the application of color for color's sake. That's clown makeup.

Think of yourself as portrait artist. Your face is your canvas. Don't be intimidated. Real natural beauty is rare. Almost everybody needs some help.

When I am filming, I am in the hands of the magic masters of makeup. Otherwise, I do my own. Okay, I sometimes go to the grocery store without makeup. I'm not *that* vain. Perhaps I should be. Whoops, too late now.

And finally this: bad makeup can give the wrong impression.

Good makeup lets the real you shine through. Now find a great outfit and hairdo and out you go.

Are you in control?
I have always tried to control my own wardrobes on stage and television. I encountered this early.

Story time! I got my first job when I was cast in *The Roaring Twenties,* a television show about, well, the Roaring Twenties — you know, Eliot Ness, Al Capone, speakeasies, machine guns, the whole bit. It was a Warner Bros. show starring Dorothy Provine.

I understood the look of the era — flapper skirts, flat hair, bad rouge. I was a theater major so I understood authenticity. None of these worked for me. None. There was no way that flapper era fringe hair was going to work on my moon face. They put me in that 'do anyway.

I was new at the studio. The makeup and hair people were great. They said, "No false eyelashes." They said my eyes were big enough. I trusted the makeup and hair people to do what would work on me. I guess I was just too new to insist.

At that time, you could never see how you looked on film before it aired, but the next week I came home and turned on my TV, and there on the *The Roaring Twenties* was an actress, Leslie Parish, wearing a long blonde flip hairstyle. The look worked well enough, but it was not of the era. But it looked swell on Leslie.

Lesson learned. I should have taken responsibility and researched that era myself and found a Roaring Twenties hair style that worked better on me. Also, I should have insisted on the false eyelashes (*everybody* else wore them).

I learned my hair would never look good in a Hollywood cut — you know, Big Hair. At my height, I would have looked like a dandelion.

When the Mary Ann role came along, Sherwood Schwartz put her in shorts, which, when you think about it, was about the only sensible thing to wear on a deserted tropical island. I packaged most of the rest.

Mary Ann got ponytails for two reasons. First, it fit her character. Second, it worked for me.

And as I look back at photos of myself, I see I often wore two ponytails from age ten through college and beyond. It worked with my face.

Those Mary Ann short shorts were a first for TV. It was a ground-breaking wardrobe long before the appearance of Daisy Dukes.

I helped design them for my body. I am not tall. I couldn't show my navel, so I designed a slight hip hugger waist, but raised it at a slight curve to cover my navel, which gave me a longer torso.

I trimmed the sides of the shorts higher on the side to make my legs look longer. No waist band. It was darted to fit. The denim was very soft. There you have it. (Question to self: what did I wear underneath?)

Previous page: A glam shot and another of sturdy little legs.

Above: From bulldog to bows. The beginning of the two ponytails . . . even then I was Mary Ann.

Opposite: The ballerina before my trick knees dislocated.

Above: Mom and me at age 10.

*Below: My first car. My stepmother's 1947 Chevy convertible before it was
repainted periwinkle blue with a plaid top and given to me on my 16th birthday.*

Miss Washington (Sharon Vaughn) and Miss Nevada competing for 1960 Miss America . . . and for the same University of Washington quarterback (Al Ferguson) whom we both dated.

Left top: Oh, dear. What to pack for the Miss America Pageant?

Bottom: Miss Nevada float in the Miss America parade, Atlantic City.

This page: (top) Contestants for Miss America, 1960, Atlantic City.

Right: Dawn with her father, Big Joe Wells.

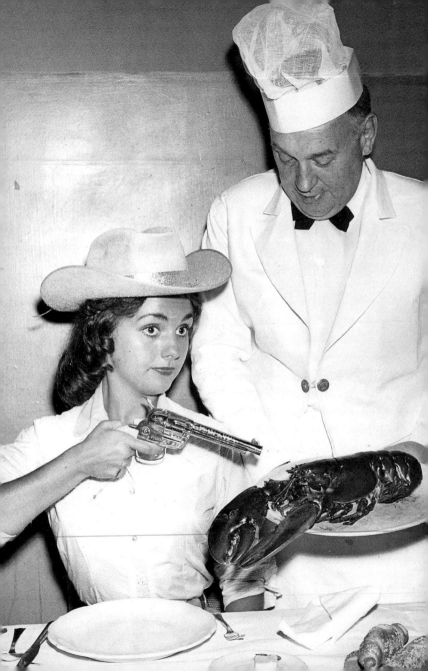

Left: Hunting for lobster,
Nevada style.

This page: Miss Nevada on
horseback.

Photos: Copyright © Dawn
Wells. All rights reserved.

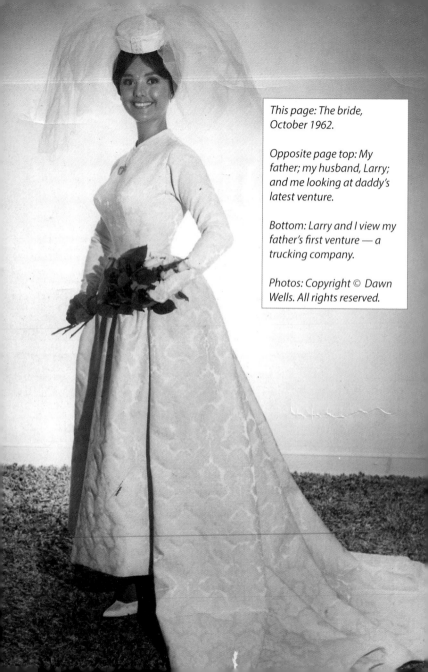

This page: The bride, October 1962.

Opposite page top: My father; my husband, Larry; and me looking at daddy's latest venture.

Bottom: Larry and I view my father's first venture — a trucking company.

My mother (left) and I were both born on October 18. My whole life my mother addressed every card or envelope with GBYILY (God Bless You I Love You).

Because she worried when I traveled, I always said, "I'll call you when I get there." The text on the tombstone, below, reflects our relationship.

Opposite page: My stepmother "Betty" (pictured with my father) was like a second mother to me. She was friends with my mother. We were all one family.

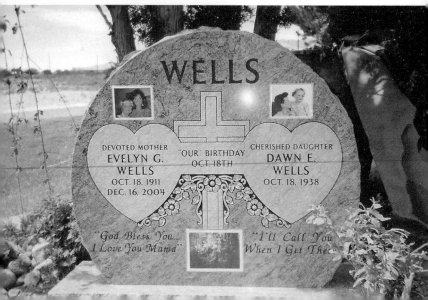

Excerpt from the funeral eulogy for Joe Wells, 1967

Who ever walked in sadness with Joe Wells? No one. You travel in happiness and laughter and you get wrapped up in that warm, wonderful, God-blessed heart and suddenly the world is a bright and wondrous place. That's the way it is with you, Joe. You live in the sunshine. And there something of a miracle here, because wherever you go the sunshine follows you and day is never dark and dreary.

You walk the happy side of the street, laugh with the sun, climb the highest mountains, ride the golden stallion, sing happy melodies of life and love and plan a bridge between those two rainbows in heaven. And you dream the most impossible dreams . . . and then you make them come true.

That's you, "Big Joe." That's why all of us say, "You're some kind of special man."

Talk about a fashionista. Where did I find the earrings to match the lapels?

Opposite page: Forever Ponytails. Mary Ann inside and out. Notice my Super 8 movie camera case over my shoulder.. I loved shooting films.

Above: Taking a gamble with Bob Denver, one of my favorite men.

Right: On the Gilligan Island set with Alan Hale, also one of my favorite men.

Photos: Copyright © Dawn Wells. All rights reserved.

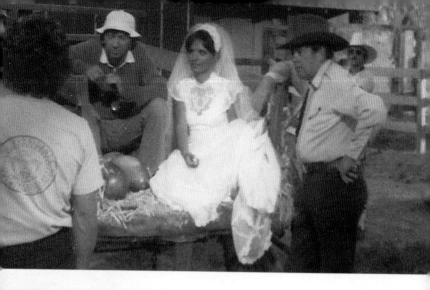

Above: More than 10 years after the series was cancelled, we reunited for television specials on CBS. It was as if we left on a Friday from work and returned on Monday, picking up where we left off. In this photo, we prepare to shoot the scene where Gilligan and the Skipper rescue me on my wedding day.

Left: It may not be a star on Hollywood Boulevard, but you can find this star in Marshfield, Mo.

Opposite page: With my husband, Larry Rosen, at Tina Louise and Les Crane's Wedding.

On the set of Rescue From Gilligan's Island.

Upper left: The Owl and the Pussycat
Lower left: Man-In-The-Moon Marigolds
Above: Dawn . . . and Dawn in It's a Mystery to Me
Photos: Copyright © Dawn Wells. All rights reserved.

This page: Except for Susie Finkle *with Roger McIntire*

Opposite right: National tour of Chapter Two *with Kathleen Gaffney.*

Bottom right: Romantic Comedy *with Patrick Wayne.*

Photos: Copyright © Dawn Wells. All rights reserved.

SEPT. 24 thru OCT. 27

Dawn
WELLS

Starring in

Same Time
Next Year

ALSO STARRING
ROGER McINTYRE

Upper left: See How They Run *with Chicago Company.*

Bottom left: Frank Wayne, Director of The Owl and the Pussycat.

Above: One of the plays I adored.

Right: Romantic Comedy

Photos: Copyright © Dawn Wells. All rights reserved.

DAWN W

STROADS DINNER THEATRE

L AND THE PUSSYCAT

THRU FEB. 26

Left: The Owl and the Pussycat
Top: Romantic Comedy *with David McCallum*
Below: National tour of Chapter Two *with David Faulkner*

This page: The Town That Dreaded Sundown

Right top: They're Playing Our Song *with Richard Ryder*

Right bottom: The Town That Dreaded Sundown

Opposite top: On the set of Roseanne, *which was shot years later on the same sound stage as* Gilligan's Island. *It was stage 2, on the CBS Radford lot.*

Opposite bottom: National tour of They're Playing Our Song

Above: Who am I? Is that a blonde femme fatale or what?

Photos: Copyright © Dawn Wells. All rights reserved.

This page: The Owl and the Pussycat

Opposite page: On the set of Winterhawk.

Photos: Copyright © Dawn Wells. All rights reserved.

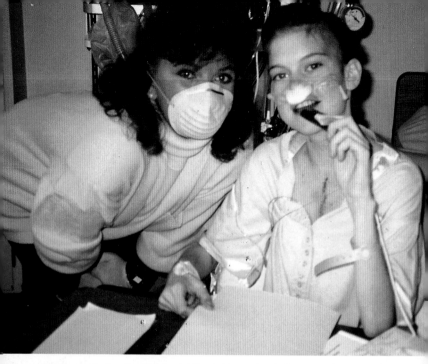

While producing the Children's Miracle Network Telethon in mid-Missouri for more than 15 years, many children touched my heart. One special child was Missy Braden.

She had suffered from cystic fibrosis since she was a small child. Our journey together gave me insight, faith, unconditional love, untapped strength, and a belief in angels.

She received a heart and lung transplant at Stanford University Hospital, with me sitting between her mother and father, who did not speak to each other.

She rallied well, counting the days until she could go outside.

She survived for about 8 months and started suffering rejection. I watched her stop fighting. I watched her belief in that it was her time. And, I watched her protect me by saying, "I will be your guardian angel."

We lost her but she is an angel on my shoulder. God has blessed you, Missy.

Here I sit in the Cloud Climber, our first donation to the Terry Lee Wells Nevada Discovery Museum. As a major donor, we are supporting our mission of focusing on woman and children of northern Nevada. I lend my name to many charities but I am most proud of serving as Chairman of the Board of my family foundation, the Terry Lee Wells Foundation.

Opposite: March of Dimes Telethon
Photos: Copyright © Dawn Wells. All rights reserved.

Photos from my climb in
Rwanda viewing the endan-
gered mountain gorillas.
Photos: Copyright © Dawn

Above: A moment with the natives from the Solomon Islands.
Below: With a member of the Australian army recovering unexploded bombs dropped in World War II. These are still dangerous. Photos: Copyright © Dawn Wells. All rights reserved.

MY SPECIAL WOODEN APPLE BOX

You can wear a wig. You can wear hair extensions. You can wear colored contact lenses. You can spray on a tan. You can girdle your midriff. You can get implants. You can get a new nose, chin, or face.

But you can only get so tall, and I am only so short. On television, even my tennis shoes had wedges. Hey, it helped. I got roles opposite Robert Conrad. I wasn't taller than he was.

Sometimes on the set of *Gilligan's Island,* you would hear someone from the crew shout "Apple Box time!"

Everyone in the Island cast was tall. Except me. Alan was about 6'4". Bobby was about 6'1". Jim, Natalie, Russell, and Tina were all taller than me.

On the set of a television show, the crew keeps what are called "apple boxes" to adjust the heights of items and people on the set. They kept a special apple box for me — it was about an inch and half tall. When you see me standing with other cast members in closeups, that's what I'm standing on.

Again the wardrobe folks were fabulous. We designed together.

The bare midriff was a look I wore in high school. It was a trend. This is a look you don't want to kid yourself about. And you probably only want to try it if you *are* a kid.

The red gingham blouse — remember Mary Ann is a farm girl from Kansas — was tied just below the bosom. It was cute and just sexy enough. I picked all the colors — powder blue, red, hot pink, Kelly green, turquoise — because they looked the best on me.

By the way, they had to match and be coordinated colors, even in black and white. When I first worked in black and white television, I was surprised to learn that clashing colors also clash in black and white. It's the difference in the shades of gray. And finally, I wore little heels to make my legs look longer.

Natalie Schafer controlled her wardrobe, too. She didn't like her ankles and you rarely saw Mrs. Howell's in dresses on *Gilligan's Island*. She was pretty and very particular and she provided great input into her wardrobe.

Most of the true style mistakes I've witnessed were made by women and girls who don't have enough knowledge about what looks best *on them*. They think they have to wear what's in the magazines. They *have* to. They force themselves into it. They give their look away to an impulse. They give it away to their…little brains. Which brings up one of the easiest ways to give it away…

What is trendy is very different from what is fashionable.

Consider fashion.
This week it's this. Next week it's that. There is nothing wrong with being trendy. When I was in high school, the trend was a cashmere sweater and socks that matched. And white buck shoes.

I wore them proudly (with a scarf around the neck). You wanted to fit in but you weren't trying to be eccentric. Luckily, that look works on just about anybody. It's when trends get eccentric that mistakes get made.

You can keep part of what's trendy and still make it work. It doesn't need to be your whole wardrobe. If you don't have the body for a miniskirt (and not that many do) don't wear one. There are other trendy items you can adopt and still be in style. You can adapt trends to you. You don't adapt yourself to trends.

Some store clerks can't help themselves.
You always get the wrong look if you don't know what *doesn't* work on you. I could never wear bell bottoms and hip huggers in the sixties and seventies. The temptation was there, though. I wanted them all! It looks so good in the store! On the display! On the mannequin! On other women!

Here is what you have to keep in mind: *Some store clerks fall in love with the inventory.* They look at it all day. They try this on. They try that on. They talk about it. They think about it. Sooner or later the inventory owns their little brains!

It's not their fault. They aren't trying to make you look awful. And the clerks, even putting aside the fact that they may work on commission, *want* you to have it.

You want the clerk who will tell you a clothing item just doesn't work for you. You want a clerk who knows your body type and style and who will sell you only those clothes that look good on you.

A good sales clerk can be a girl's best friend — shoot, she may even give you a call when the store receives something that she thinks would look great on you. Seek her out . . . and don't let her go. You can find one in each of your favorite shops.

It's great to have someone you trust when you shop for clothes and accessories. Someone who will really tell you what you look like from behind. Someone who won't ignore your muffin top. Someone will say flat out, "You don't have the body for a mini-skirt." Someone who will stand in as your Big Brain.

It's not a question of "Is this dress in style?"

Here's a lesson I got from my mother. She didn't care about fashion. She cared about me. She would ask, "Are you really going to wear your hair that way?" She wasn't critiquing modern hairstyles that were beyond her generation. She was telling me that I was turning my looks over a to a fad and that it didn't work for me.

Study yourself. Know your body type. Even great bodies don't look great in everything. It's an illusion. An expression of who you are. It's how you want the world to see you. It's how you feel. Make it work for *you*. You will always feel confident if it fits your way.

Beware! As you age, your body may change. And if that does happen, the last thing you want to do is cling to your old look. I concentrate on what looks good on *me*. I learned by trial and error and honest evaluation of what styles would work for me. There will *always* be some styles that won't work on you.

You have to discover what your look, your image, is.

It doesn't happen overnight. Once you have it, then you have to maintain it and let it grow with you. I knew a woman who you would describe as a phenomenal dresser. Style! Flair! Fit! She bought her entire wardrobe at Goodwill. She had the flair and confidence to carry it off.

Not everybody finds their look. Wait. That's not quite right. Everybody finds a look. Maybe, though, it isn't the right look for them. Finding your look requires effort and genuine thought and experimentation.

Story time! I was told that before Marilyn Monroe left the house, she quickly turned around and noted the first thing that caught her eye in the mirror. She would remove it.

I was also told that Audrey Hepburn ate with a tight belt around her waist, so she wouldn't eat too much. We can control how we look to others if we choose to.

There is so much influence from media and so much of it is misplaced. I've said it before: If you saw it on television, it didn't really happen.

Take Mary Ann's character outfit. It was designed for television. It wasn't designed for life. The short shorts, needless to say, were daring for the time. I was self-conscious. I was not one to flaunt. Between takes I wore a sweatshirt around my waist. The crew on the *Gilligan's Island* set teased me. They called me "Bubble Butt."

Bubble Butt was a great look for the camera. It didn't quite work in the cafeteria.

Your voice.

Yes, your voice is part of your style — as much as how your are dressed or groomed. Your voice is more important than you realize. I thought Mary Ann's voice was a little high. After *Gilligan's Island,* I lowered it some and made more it more resonant.

I listened to myself. I also thought my voice was a bit too monotone. I used a tape recorder. I tried reading scripts in different voices. I tried to give myself as much variation and range as possible.

All this training led to voice work , which I love. You can be anything. Nobody sees you. A king, a queen, or a koala. A little girl or a sex kitten.

Story time! I was asked to be the narrator of the motion picture *Winter Hawk*, which was unusual for a woman then. What a thrill and what an unusual creative experience. I recorded the narration as the composer adjusted to what I said. It was like a duet. The result? The music ebbed and swelled and made my narration richer. It was an inspiring process. And rare.

You don't have to have the voice you are born with. You can warm up a squeaky voice. You can turn down the volume on a loud voice. It is fairly simple to analyze your own voice. Does it have too much of one thing? Is that one thing pleasant?

Coming from Nevada, I didn't have to work my way out of a strong regional accent that would be jarring on television. I don't think accents are a bad thing, it is just something that you should be aware of. Fran Drescher turned her accent into an asset!

SHE TAUGHT ME BEAUTY 101

I was relatively new to TV when I was cast in *Gilligan's Island*.

While shooting the show, I learned so much by observing Tina. She knew exactly what she was doing. Tina taught me makeup and camera angles. She was already a Broadway and Hollywood star. She was voluptuous and gorgeous. This isn't news, just have a look at a rerun of *Gilligan's Island*.

Tina was terribly disciplined about her looks. She always carried a parasol in the sun. I never saw her eat anything "bad." She was very aware of her looks and how she came across on television. She knew every flattering camera angle. She preferred to be shot on her left side. I thought she was beautiful from both sides.

I was grateful for her assistance. There was never any animosity or jealousy between us. There was no competition between us. She even ordered mink eyelashes for us from New York.

Don't mumble. People who mumble deliver one of two messages:
1. I know you aren't listening.
2. I don't care if you are listening.

It is pointless to say something in a way that cannot be understood. Think about what kind of image you project when you speak unclearly.

Think of your voice as a musical instrument. Is it soft enough? Is it loud enough? Is it sweet enough? Is it powerful enough? Does it hit the right notes? Do people want to hear it? You can work on your voice, your range and clarity, but you have to *want to*.

Does a $500 purse make you a better person?

Is a $500 purse extravagant if you have $500 to blow? I guess not. I'm also guessing that most readers of this book don't have $500 to just blow. I don't. So, I'll use it as standard.

The $500 purse is a double whammy. It represents Vanity and also what we used to call External Validation. Vanity *comes* from your little brain. External Validation *speaks* to your little brain. I think we all know what Vanity is. What about External Validation?

Story time! Minnie Pearl was an absolutely delightful comic. She worked the country and western circuit — the Grand Ole Opry, Hee Haw. Her trademark was a gaudy storebought hat *with the price tag still dangling from it.* Now, that's External Validation! In her day it was a cheap hillbilly hat. Today, we sport the Louis Vuitton bag, or it's a shirt with a label to be noticed, or it's *those* shoes and *only* those shoes.

External Validation can be difficult to avoid. Not to pick on Louis Vuitton, but . . . why? It's the same pattern year in and year out. It's the same color. Thousands of cheap knockoffs are sold to people who *know* they are cheap knockoffs.

What, other than External Validation, would possess you to buy a cheap copy of a brand? You end up toting a lousy bag that falls apart on you, logo and all.

Why do you want to wear an item of clothing with another

person's name on it? Does Tommy Hilfiger have a shirt with Dawn Wells emblazoned on it? I don't think so. Hmmm. Maybe I should ask him.

The scales don't lie.
In show business, you have to "make weight." You can't be cast in a role at one weight and then show up for shooting at twenty pounds heavier. Weight is part of the job just as much as knowing your lines.

We live in a culture of plenty. It is so easy to put some of that plenty on your waistline. Yes, you have a genetic profile. Some people gain weight faster than others, or not at all. So what? It doesn't change the problem. My father was 6'4"and weighed 250 pounds. My mother was 5'1" and maybe 90 pounds. That doesn't mean it's okay for me to be 5'1" and 250 pounds.

Your looks are not worth your health.

This little section is about weight and the desire or the need to control it. Pause button here. I need to go into full lecture mode. If you have ever considered or if you are currently considering the purchase of a weight loss supplement, here are three things to do with your money that I promise you will be just as useful to you:

1. Set fire to it.
2. Throw it out the window.
3. Give it away.
Is there anything, *anything* more precisely designed to appeal to your little brain than weight loss schemes? Stop. I'll answer: No.

Ask yourself, where do weight loss schemes go when they disappear?

Okay, I need to clarify. I don't want to confuse diets with diet pills. Diets may or may not work. Good healthy diets usually do work. I'm no expert. This is just what I've seen over the years. Personally, I've never used the crazy ones, like fasting or extreme use of supplements. Okay, pause button off.

The point is: Your weight can force you into bad decisions. One of the most stylish traits you can have is to be comfortable in your clothes. When you feel good about yourself you look better. If you are comfortable in your clothes you feel good about yourself. It's a mindset.

Of course, you feel good in your old sweats. (Note to self: do I really look good in these?)

Large doesn't mean fat. Not all people are made to be 5'6" inches tall and weigh 120 pounds. Some people are just built larger, but it doesn't mean fat and that you can't be stylish and attractive. However, if you are large, keep that blouse tucked in. Casual turns into sloppy way too fast on large women.

When you are healthy it shows in your smile, your teeth, your clear eyes, your skin, and your disposition. All are part of your beauty.

Your style is a package. How clean is the package? How groomed is it? Clean hair. Clean teeth. Clean body. Clean mind. And laundered clothes. We are blessed with inexpensive products designed to keep us clean and presentable. They fill entire grocery store aisles! They fill entire stores! Go there! Everybody on the elevator will thank you.

Know how to use the tools.
You know, you can make yourself more beautiful just by making yourself more presentable. Oprah Winfrey always said that the best thing that ever happened to women was hair dye. You don't have to be gray unless you want to. You never have to unless you want to. You don't have to show your age.

I developed acne in the sixth grade. (Girls with good skin have no idea.) My mother took me to a dermatologist. I began wearing prescription medicated makeup. I was the only one wearing makeup in my class.

There are very few people who are so exceptionally beautiful that they couldn't use some improvement.

I was once told that when applied correctly, one should not be able to tell you are wearing make-up. The only time your make-up might be more noticed is for a formal occasion - a black tie event. Make-up should be applied to enhance the nature in you, not necessarily recreate it.

For me, the best use for makeup is to enhance your best feature. Everybody has one. I think applying makeup is an art. I think every woman is a different canvas. I

f you want to wear makeup, you should put as much attention toward developing your skills as a painter does. You've got a powder brush. He's got a paint brush. You should also be as self-critical as an artist. Once again, you need a trusted friend to tell you if it isn't working.

Sometimes, even a brother might help.

You can't just paste it on, though. Okay, it's a cliché to say that women glow from the inside. That health and confidence and maturity create beauty. Well, it's also true.

I used to think plastic surgery was a bad idea. Now, I don't know. It has gotten so sophisticated. It seems to me that plastic surgery hurts you when your little brain starts calling the shots. It gets to be like rearranging furniture. Everything needs a tuck and a pull.

At the same time, plastic surgery can be healing. It can make you finally enjoy the person in the mirror. I don't know. If you think something is really wrong with you — your nose, your chin —if it can make you feel better about what you present to the world, then, well, please just use your Big Brain. If you're a 34b and you want to be a 36c, or vice versa, thats your choice. The opportunity is there. And once you've done the research and consultation, okay, but not at too young an age. Not too much, not too often, not too young.

Let the world see your smile.
I'm not talking about the condition of your teeth, here. I'm talking about the condition of your personality. Of you. Try as you might, you can't apply a personality. It doesn't come out of a jar. However, you can put on a smile. What's that song from *Annie* — "You're Never Really Dressed Without a Smile?"

Your smile is your biggest fashion accessory. Forget — please forget — the "model glare." You know, that posed, semi-fierce look that comes from pages of magazines. I've never known what it is supposed to say. "Hey, I look great in Versace and also I just cured the common cold." Enough with the Fashion Squint. Smile!

My mother always said you attract more flies with honey than with vinegar. I've always remembered that, although I wish she hadn't used flies. The point is, personal warmth is attractive. It glows. A smile offers a look inside you. It turns on the glow. I don't care where you bought that dress or how much you spent on your hair or how unusual those new pumps are, if your face looks like you are stuck in jury duty, they don't matter.

Here is where we get to the heart of the matter. You can put on a smile, but if you put on a fake one, well, why bother? The smile isn't part of your persona. It isn't your style. It's what lies beneath the smile. Fake smiles aren't attractive. Fake smiles make people want to run the other way.

There's much in life that can give you a smile — you just have to be willing to use your eyes to see it.

Good looks can't overcome bad breath.
Never ever, ever, ever (three evers!) turn down a mint.

Dangerous choices.
It was a good thing that the censors put a ruler on Ginger's cleavage, not that Tina was prone to excess. It was a visible reminder of a basic style standard. Too much of a good thing is still too much, especially if you are the only who considers it good.

You live in a fashion world of dangerous choices. I'm thinking visible thong underwear here. I'm thinking skimpy halter tops and tees. Don't get me started on rear end cleavage.

What you show and how you show it defines you. You need to ask this question: Do people really want to see this? Do they want to see bowling ball cleavage? Do they want see your bare muffin top? Answers: No. And no.

You hear people say, "The human body is beautiful." Uh, okay, I guess. Michelangelo thought it was. On the other hand, Michelangelo never spent a day at the beach in 2014.

There are some things that should never, ever come near spandex, especially spandex in small stretches. Cover yourself!

How many style points do you get?
In some Olympic sports you get a basic score and then you get style points, or a style score. I'm thinking figure skating here. Well, how many style points would you give yourself?

I know you are under pressure to look a certain way in order to be accepted. I know the pressure mostly comes from inside you. I know the influences of media and advertising add to the pressure. Don't try to total up your style points using pressure points.

Look at yourself objectively. Be your own judge. Do you get style points for your smile? Do you get style points for your grooming? Do you get style points for your posture and voice and sense of place? Your fitness? Your attitude? Notice that none of these style points can be purchased in a store.

Caps

No caps

MY "COCAINE" TEETH

For many years I used temporary teeth caps. They covered my two small teeth near the front. Otherwise I looked like a squirrel or a beaver, especially with my chubby cheeks.

Many a time I forgot they were in my mouth and chewed them up when I took a bite of something, so I resorted to carrying them in a tiny vial that I tucked in my bra. Just before the cameras rolled, I would turn my back, put them in, and do the scene.

One day while filming *Return to Gilligan's Island,* the assistant director came and said, "Please, Dawn, will you do me a favor? Don't turn around and put in your teeth. When you turn back around smiling, the fans in the studio audience keep asking me if you are sniffing cocaine."

Ten years after *Gilligan's Island* was off the air I had four teeth pulled and wore braces for two years.

You have your own template. Enjoy.
Once you have found a style that works for you, the fun begins. You aren't shopping anymore. You are hunting. You can experiment. Don't tell yourself you don't have a knack for putting things together.

Develop the knack! There is no template. You can be a little eccentric. You can have your own identity. What looks best on you isn't necessarily fashion. You can make beauty out of anything. Yes, you are free!

The real you is your style. Your generosity. Your contentment. Your empathy. A friend of mine once observed that people who are doing the work they enjoy are handsome.

Handsome. That was his word. He meant it as a description for both men and women. I instantly knew what he meant. It's an aura. It's the inner you working silently all around you. It's your style.

Be handsome.

If you still insist on wearing pajama bottoms on the plane, well, I can't help you.

MARY ANN'S TERRIBLE TOO'S

Too gaudy

Too tight

Too revealing

Too cheesy

Too trashy

Too chi chi

Too affected

Too unnatural

Too contrived

Too ornate

Illustration by James Bennett

parentage

fam • i • ly

noun

: a group of people who are related to each other

friend

noun

: a person who you like and enjoy being with

HOUSEHOLD

COMPANIONS

PALS

FATHER

MOTHER

generations

HUSBAND

WIFE

MATES

sidekick

To be with those you love
Friends, family, and the "Road to Special"

When your mother asks, "Do you want a piece of advice?" it's a mere formality. It doesn't matter if you answer yes or no. You're going to get it anyway.

— Erma Bombeck

I was already very much Mary Ann when I auditioned for the *Gilligan's Island* role — the work ethic, the values, the study habits. I got those from my parents.

Lucky for me, Sherwood Schwartz, who created *Gilligan's Island*, wanted a girl like that to be the voice of reason on the island.

I think Sherwood really had a vision when he created *Gilligan's Island*. He created a family of misfits, not relatives. Everything Sherwood did had a family feel to it. He followed *Gilligan's Island* by creating *The Brady Bunch*.

His own family was old fashioned and it came through in his writing. I feel privileged to be part of that company.

Why would a silly show about seven misfits on an island have such staying power? Because it was about family trying to live together in harmony.

If I had grown up without love, I don't know what I would be.

Where did my talent (assuming I have any) come from? I would have to say my family. I grew up with my mother in Reno, Nevada. I spent a great deal of time with my father in Las Vegas, which was 400 or so miles south. Reno was just across the California border at the foot of the Sierra Nevada Mountains and gambling was legal — and most, if not all of the vices you can associate with a gambling town in the Fifties were there in spades.

Actually, that's not quite right. I grew up in two Renos. There was the Reno of bright lights and glitz and gambling and prostitution and quick divorces. There was also the Reno of normal, middle class suburbs and suburban family values and an award-winning high school — one of the top schools in the country at the time. I really grew up in the second Reno, even as I observed the glitz of the other Reno.

My family had western roots. My great-great-grandfather drove a stagecoach in the gold rush of 1849. My grandmother on my mother's side, Rose, made her piano debut when she was nine at Piper's Opera House in Virginia City. It was a real gold rush boomtown. It's been a ghost town, but today there is a resurgence of mining there.

Grammie Rose could compose music, paint, play the piano, and design and sew clothing. She was the artist in the family.

My father was larger than life, even by Las Vegas standards. He was physically imposing — 6′4″ and 250 pounds — and a hale fellow, well met. He was gentle, successful, and smart. He never met a stranger. My father was self-made and bore the confidence of a self-made man. He showed it early. When he was a schoolboy, his mother made a mistake with a load of wash and all the trousers came out pink. His brothers refused to wear them to school. He said, "Give them to me, mom. I'll wear them and dare them to tease me."

My father was a very kind and giving man. They called him Big Joe Wells. He had a heart the size of Nevada. He was even asked to run for governor of Nevada. They said, "But which party, Joe?"

One of my father's good friends and a regular in his household was Rex Bell. Along with being a Western movie star and the husband of Clara Bowe, he was lieutenant governor of Nevada.

There's the difference between Las Vegas and Reno. It was two lives for me. My father had an expansive house and a stable. My mother and I lived in a small tract house near my high school in Reno. My father had quite a large household staff. My mother never even wanted a gardener. Stars and VIPs passed through my father's home in Vegas. The governor never visited our house in Reno.

Knowing these two worlds was a gift to me. It gave me perspective. There was respect between my two households and love resided there. Between my mother, my father, my stepmother, and my brother and sister . . . and me. Wait! Include the in-laws, too.

We used to say you never knew who my father would bring home — a homeless guy off the street or the governor. Before he was a co-founder of the Thunderbird Hotel on the Las Vegas strip, my father established his first success by starting a trucking company, Wells Cargo, which then grew into a highway construction company and a mining company with interests even in Peru and Turkey.

On the day of my father's funeral, the federal courts in Las Vegas were closed. It was the first time this gesture had ever been made for someone who was not a judge.

Here's a story that was told by my grandmother Wells. When my father was a child about the age of 6 or 7, he was very late coming home from school, which, of course, worried the family. When he arrived, my grandmother scolded him and wanted to know where he had been. He answered, "I was following a bee and I wanted to see where he lived."

My mother was as straight-laced as she was small (she stood barely over five feet). She was smart. Very smart. Even though her father wouldn't let her go to college, she became a professional bookkeeper and worked until she was 72.

My mother met my father when he applied for credit at the Reno Chevrolet dealership where she worked as a bookkeeper. She tried to talk her boss out of giving him credit (she got nowhere). Ah, it all started from there.

My parents divorced when I was four, but I never felt I grew up in a broken home. I never heard a bad word about my parents from either one of them. My parents remained close after the divorce and throughout their lives and were in sync about how I was to be raised. When my father remarried, my stepmother, Betty, and my mother became friends. They, too, were in sync about me. I lived with my mother, but I grew up surrounded by love in two homes.

I didn't grow up in a divided family. I grew up in separate families. We celebrated holidays together. It was two families as one. Imagine that. Not easy, I assume. I never saw any discord. It wasn't a competition. It was about raising me right.

I lived as an only child with my mother. It was just the two of us in our little house. Of the many things I learned from my mother, two stand out: Her independence and her discipline. Oops. Don't forget her genius in the kitchen.

She was a wonderful homemaker and an excellent bookkeeper for five pediatricians at the same time. She devoted her life to me. No matter how hard she worked, she was there when I got home each day.

She never lectured me about manners. I was taught by example. She watched me like a hawk. She loved me and I came first in her life.

We had a nice, small house. She bought it. She cooked, she cleaned, she gardened. There were always fresh vegetables on our table. She was a homemaker. She was a Brownie leader. She taught me independence. She worked five days a week and I never saw her go on a date. She thought my father was a great man and a great father and she didn't want me to have a stepfather.

Story time! My mother was a world-class worrier. That is *not* an overstatement! When I was a junior in college, my sweetheart was a quarterback for the University of Washington football team. He wanted to drive me from Reno back to the University of Washington in Seattle. My mother didn't want me in the car with a boy for that length of time, but she let me go.

While we were driving through Oregon, a highway patrol car pulled us over. The patrolman approached the car and asked, "Is there a Dawn Wells in this car?" I said I was. The patrolman said, "Call your mother."

Another one! I was 65 years old, walking through an airport in Australia. A pilot walked up to me. "Are you Dawn Wells?" "Yes." "Your mother has been looking for you all day."

My father died early and suddenly in a bungled procedure at a hospital. My mother had never remarried. I think she never stopped loving my father. There was a bond. They were more like a brother and sister.

She lived a long and full life. She moved to Los Angeles to be with me. She got a job with the county. (Note to self: never forget her being turned down for a job in a doctor's office when he said, "Why are you applying for this job? I need a tall, good-looking blonde.")

When I fell in love and moved to Nashville, my mother moved there as well. When I fell out of love, I moved back to California and she moved to the Gulf Shores of Florida. She managed my beach property for me and she loved it. I still see that little five-foot-tall woman walking the beach to this day.

She developed macular degeneration and almost lost her eyesight. That's when she moved into my guest house in California. She never lost her mental capacity.

She did not raise me with an iron fist. She raised me with an iron mind. She was very strong, independent, smart, and capable. She was fair, disciplined, and she gave lots of love as a great foundation. She was very difficult at times. She taught me that very well.

My mother and I shared the same birthday. She always made the same cake for me every year (and only on our birthday) and would ship it wherever I was. On her last birthday with me — she was 93 — she said, "It's getting kind of late. Let's make the cake together." We did. I still miss her.

My family is still with me in many ways, large and small. I still use my grandmother's spoon in the kitchen. I have cookware that was my mother's. I use an old tin pot that *always* has been in my family. Is an old tin pot an antique? Well, not in the sense that it has value in a shop. It's just a wonderful thing that carries along from generation to generation. A connection. A continuity. These things have meaning. Be careful before you discard them.

During our last Thanksgiving together, my mother was making cranberry sauce from scratch and decided it was time I learned how. As I made the sauce, she insisted I was doing it wrong. "It is not going to jell, Dawn." Well, me being overly confident, I said, "Of course it will jell." We had quite an argument. In the end, it jelled. I still have that extra package of raw cranberries in my freezer from that day so many years ago. Well, I turned out to be right that day, but . . .

Your mother is not always wrong.

I am not a mother. I am not trying to be your mother. I am absolutely not trying to tell your mother how to be a mother!!! . . . three exclamation points *again*. I can only speak to you as someone who had a mother. Can we agree that we all have that in common? In an earlier chapter of this book I said, "I'll be the scout. You be the wagon train." I've been there. I've seen it. I've made the mistakes. I've learned from them (I hope).

Well, where do you think your mother was all those years before you came along? Was she just waiting to be your mother? No! She was out there. She led a life. She saw it. She made mistakes. She learned from them (she hopes).

Your mother has many jobs. One of them is to tell you Things You Don't Want to Hear. While all the world around you is whispering into your little brain, your mother wants to talk with your Big Brain.

What you may see as a taskmaster, an oppressive ruler, an authority without authority is, in fact ,a woman expressing unconditional love. Yes, she has the right to go through your private things, to search your drawers, to look under your bed, to monitor your social media. You are not bulletproof. You don't understand that. She does. And she has the authority to say so.

You don't know everything. Wait, that's not it. You have not yet had to apply what you think you know to the real world. You don't know if it will work, which makes it way to easy to assume it will.

Let me tell you, just about anything sounds like it will work until you try it. What's that old saying? "For every complex problem there is a solution that is clear, simple, and wrong." You aren't stupid. You are inexperienced. You are really the opposite of stupid. The very essence of stupid is *experience without learning.*

Finding what is real.

So much of Hollywood drama and comedy depends upon dysfunctional families, you'd think there is an epidemic of flawed people. If you start getting the idea that this is the norm, well, take it from your scout, it isn't.

My three families.

I have had varied roles in raising children. They were not my own. My first family included a stepbrother and stepsister who were adopted by my father and his second wife. In my second family, I was a stepmother in spirit to two girls. In my third family, I was honored to be a godmother. And now there are grandchildren.

A surrogate mother.
My father was married four times. He and his last wife, Betty, adopted two kids — a daughter, Weslee, and a son, Joe Carson (Kit) — when I was fifteen. They lived in Las Vegas. When I went to visit when they were little, I played with them like they were my dolls. I was more like an aunt than a sister. I never shared a home with them.

That all changed after my father died suddenly and Betty became ill. I became a sort of surrogate mother for the kids when they were twelve and thirteen years old. Along with my mother, we shared in some of the raising of Weslee and Kit until they became adults. Kit has since passed away. Weslee has raised her three sons and Kit's daughter. It's a great family, and really, the only immediate family I have on my family tree.

A stepmother in spirit.
I was blessed to be in a relationship with a wonderful man for fifteen years. Tom lived in Nashville. We never married. We never lived together, but I was committed enough to move to Nashville and then move my mother to Nashville and buy her a house there.

Tom had two delightful daughters, Kim and Julie. Tom and I and the girls' mother, Pat, brought those two girls through the "terrible teens." Pat and I were friendly. There was a mutual respect.

I am still very much a part of the lives of Kim and Julie. They say you don't get to choose your family. Well, in a way I did. I couldn't have chosen a better one. And now, Julie has fabulous children of her own — Amy, Elizabeth, and Austin. I am especially close to Kim and to Amy, who now has an adopted son.

Tom's brother had Down Syndrome. His mother suffered from Alzheimer's and was in a nursing home for eleven years. I was there for him and for them. They were all a very important part of my life. I think of them as my family.

A Godmother.
My dear friend Gail shared her very special children with me.

Perhaps you recall the story of Jimmy — the boy who was brain damaged as a baby — from the earlier chapter on Optimism. Jim (only I call him Jimmy) is Gail's son. Jimmy has a sister, Cindy, who is deaf.

I learned so much from Gail. She refused to see her children as "different." She and her children have succeeded against the odds. They are the best they can be. Today, Cindy has children of her own, too. She is a fabulous mother. She uses a hearing dog. I am the godmother of her oldest son, Matthew. I think of Cindy as the daughter I never had. I am so proud to be associated with her family.

Mother of my mother.
In her later years, my mother came to live with me. Slowly, our roles reversed. It was a privileged time for me. I am so fortunate. It was my turn to give back to her. I now understand unconditional love.

On the other hand . . .

It's not like I can't see the genuine problems. I've seen dysfunction. Divorce, blended families, single mothers. I think it is more accurate to say there is a bit of dysfunction in every family.

I call mine a *great* dysfunctional family, just out of the normal world. It's a *perfect* dysfunctional family.

You can find yourself in an environment where there *is* authority without authority, or worse, no authority, and you so young. You didn't choose this world. It's a world you never made. This is awful for you. It can leave you to grow on your own. It can make you vulnerable.

Let's say you are on your own. You are forced to be your own guide, your own leader, your own scout. If you choose to listen and look, you are assaulted, and I mean *assaulted*, by cultural messages that tell you to behave pretty much as you please. Notice, please, I said, *"If you choose to listen and look."*

It's so easy to look only at the world that is right in front of your eyes, especially if that world is on a television or movie screen. That world isn't real. It isn't truth. It isn't history. It isn't normal. It can't be normal. It is made up, concocted, fabricated to fit neatly into a little rectangle. Your life doesn't fit into a little rectangle. Don't let others set your boundaries. Look past the rectangle. The same goes with what you hear.

If you don't have parental guidance and you are on your own, you must make the same demand on this world that my mother made of me, "Think it through. Convince me you are right."

Bring the debater in you to life every day. Ask yourself these questions.

What is the point of doing this?
What is the benefit?
Where does it get me?
What's the other side?
What's the worst that can happen?

Look at both sides. Prove claims of truth. If you lack parental guidance, *you* weigh the answers to these questions. In the absence of parental guidance, you must be in charge of your surroundings as much as possible. You must find mentors. You must find people you trust. You must understand that you really do need guidance. We can begin with…

Your friends are not always right.

Here is a Dawn Rule of Thumb: If you are in a room and everybody in the room is in total agreement with you, then you are in the wrong room.

Are your friends debaters?
Do they think independently?
Are you their devil's advocate?
Who is your devil's advocate?
Do you learn from your friends?
Is what you learn of any real value?
What is the value of your friendships?

Are your friends real? Hmmm. Why do I ask? If you have a thousand social media friends, you *don't* have a thousand friends. C'mon, do you really need Mary Ann to clue you in on that one?

Friendship runs deep in your life. Your friends can be male or female, young or old. You can have friends for a reason, a season, or a lifetime. Friendships create bonds that withstand separation. You can have a friend for a season and see her years later, and the bond is still there. You know what they say, "Friends are the family you get to choose."

Who to choose? Who will choose you? We live in a world where you have to decide which friends are real. So, what is a real friend?

Well, here are Mary Ann's thoughts on the matter:

Cliques are not friendships.
The motivations are wrong. Look, you can't *belong* to a friendship. True friendships are formed by attraction, like magnets. They are not formed by repulsion, by shutting out, by closing doors or turning backs. Friends don't turn backs, they have your back. True friendships are formed by appreciation. They are not formed by criticism. Cliques tend to have leaders. The leader establishes the behavior of the clique. Leaders expect followers to behave like followers. Egad! Here you are chafing at the authority of your parents and accepting the authority of…what, some bossy kid? True friendship is above peer pressure. True friendship never asks you to sacrifice the inner you.

Sisterhood is essential.
Sisterhood is good for the soul. We talked about male friends in an earlier chapter. Now, it's time to embrace…well, ourselves. Sisterhood is a safe haven. The commonality of sisterhood is common interests and goals and common observations. Sisterhood is good for the mind and heart. It is, really, the opposite of a clique. It isn't a surface. It is deeper.

You can't really want to belong to a sisterhood, either. It isn't an existing thing where you knock on the door and ask if you can come in. Sisterhood grows around you. It evolves. All of a sudden, there it is! You hardly bother to ask how it was formed. You never have to sacrifice the inner you to be in a sisterhood. You never have to adjust your standards or morals. Sisterhood is your Big Brain. Cliques are your little brain.

Envy doesn't equal popularity.
You don't have to be the center of attention to be popular. You don't need to have things that other people desire — looks, clothes, cars, club memberships, whatever. You'll never be popular trying to make people want to like you or worse, *be* like you. Wanting, trying, to be popular may just be the quickest way to make yourself unpopular.

You can't grow popularity.
You can't harvest it.
You certainly can't store it so you can use it later.

Popularity grows on you by itself. How? People are attracted to people who take a genuine interest in them. Emphasis on the word *genuine*. It's that simple.

If you can sincerely demonstrate for your friends that you understand their worth and potential — that you think they are important — and *if you are kind to your friends and if you treat them as equals, you will be popular.*

Here's the best part. Even as your popularity grows, you will never think of yourself as popular. This is because you become popular by not thinking of yourself. At the same time, there is nothing wrong with wanting to be a cheerleader. Just keep in mind how silly you'd look if there was nobody in the stands.

It is awful to feel like an outcast.

If you are reading this and you feel shunned and insecure, if you feel you don't belong anywhere, I beg you to understand: If you feel that life somehow manages to never include you, *this too shall pass.* There *is* a place for you. The single hardest thing to get across to young people is just how temporary most of the life that surrounds you right now is. You can feel like you are in a canoe in the rapids and there is no end. You can feel like the water will never slow down and be calm. It will. You are in a time of discovery. When you arrive on the other side of the rapids, you will not be the same person you are today.

Will the new person be a better person? That's up to you. It also depends on whom you associate with. It's a good idea to keep in mind that fringe groups and gangs exist for people who believe themselves to be alone.

Think about it, a group of loners. It is so easy to be drawn into this if you feel alone, too. Well, keep in mind that gangs and fringe groups are no different than cliques. The same rules apply. They have leaders and followers. They have rules you must obey. The group is only interested in you insofar as you benefit the group. It's a one-way deal. The group is asking for *you* to disappear. The group doesn't want you to come out of the rapids as a better person because the group knows the better person won't stick around. Most important, who is doing the thinking in a gang or a fringe group? Let's say you are in one? Who is the devil's advocate? Look around. Do you see one? I thought so. Do you see any Big Brains working? I thought so. In which case, why isn't your Big Brain working?

The lessons of seven castaways.

We are surrounded by imperfect people. We get along by navigating those imperfections. That's what the castaways on *Gilligan's Island* did every week. The castaways didn't choose each other. The castaways didn't start the "three-hour tour" as friends. The castaways had one common bond thrust upon them, of course. They were stuck together on an island. If it had stopped there, the scriptwriters would have given up on the second episode. The castaways found other common bonds. They discovered new tolerances within themselves. There were no outcasts. There were no grudges.

Being marooned on an island with no chance of escape may be the last place on Earth anybody would want to be. The castaways made this last place on earth a safe haven for humanity. The castaways somehow made a tiny place larger — big enough for all of them. The castaways understood there was life on the other side of the island. They talked about it. They hoped for it. They planned for it. There was no despair. That's what friends and family can do for you. They can brighten your darkest hour. And you theirs.

A personal note about my family & friends:

I have a sister, nieces, nephews, cousins, and three surrogate families, so to speak. My family consists of not only blood relatives but the people who became the nucleus of my life. Some are genetic, some by chance, some by choice, all ages, all genders, some near, and some far. Each fills a special need. Some more than others. I do not come from a large family; I never lived with brothers or sisters, but I learned to share and co-exist in harmony with those whom I share my life.

My Reno high school friends are my lifelong friends. So are my classmates at Stephens College, University of Washington, Alpha Chi Omega sorority, co-stars and neighbors. Some of my most extraordinary experiences have been adventures with incredible women from my alma maters: a gorilla climb in Rwanda, African safaris, fly fishing around the world and canoeing through the Solomon Islands with no running water or electricity. Sharing these experiences are the facets of my life. They are the sum of who I am and always becoming. These are valued friends for a lifetime! BFF? Isn't that how the techies say it? Best Friends Forever?

MARY ANN'S TERRIBLE TOO'S

Too friendless

Too isolated

Too empty

Too apart

Too estranged

Too afraid

Too rejected

Too shy

Too alienated

Too lonesome

Illustration by James Bennett

Sherwood Schwartz and hand-carved cast. Photo: Dawn Wells Archives

A FAMILY OF FRIENDS

A studio lot is an intimate world. You develop family habits. For instance, Bob Denver and I developed the habit of speaking fast when we were in a scene together. It got faster and faster. Our director, Les Goodwin, said, "You two could do a thirty-minute sitcom in fifteen minutes. You talk so fast." One Christmas, Bobby decided he'd find a tiny island we could all buy and give each part of the crew a little part of it. It didn't happen because Thurston wanted to buy liquor, instead. The miser! :-)

In a way, we became a miniature family within that working environment. Alan, Russell, and I were very close. Later, Natalie Schafer and I became so close, I was like the daughter she never had. Bobby and I had a very special bond, too. I was privileged to be invited to his home. We filled niches for each other. Odd, but it was the opposite of being marooned. We weren't isolated or alone. We had each other.

performance

work

noun

: a job or activity that you do regularly especially in order to earn money
: the things that you do as part of your job

Exertion

INDUSTRY

striving

They call it the work ethic, not the work theory

Without ambition one starts nothing. Without work one finishes nothing. The prize will not be sent to you. You have to win it.
— Ralph Waldo Emerson

Maynard G. Krebs got more out of the word "work" than anyone on television, before or since. It was the late 1950s. Maynard was Bob Denver's first major television role in the *The Many Loves of Dobie Gillis.*

The "work" thing was a standing bit. The Maynard character was what was at the time called a beatnik. Today, we might call him a slacker. Whenever the word "work" was spoken in his presence, he repeated the word in a fearful yelp along with a twitch. I can still hear Bobby's voice.

I always liked that about the Maynard character. It was one of those rare comic bits that get funnier with repetition. I marveled at Bobby on the set after he became Gilligan. It came from inside . . . no rehearsal. He just became Gilligan. When they said, "Action," he just did it.

A television set is a good place to witness the world of work at it's best. Just a few minutes of film requires a ton of people. Just watch the credits roll on a movie or TV show. For every actor on screen, there are dozens, even hundreds of people on the other side of the camera.

It is like a football team. If everybody on the team doesn't do the job on each play, the ball never moves. I love the teamwork that acting requires. It's magic when it works. It works when we pay attention and we give and we understand the level of responsibility of everyone on set, right down to the food service.

I think that's the beauty of work. You rarely do it alone. You have to work together. You have to want to work. I think this is a very American trait, and a very good one.

The arts can seem glamorous. The process can seem easy. That's because the whole idea is to make it look easy. It is work. Do you think every singer wakes up every day wanting to sing? Every painter wanting to paint? Every musician wanting to play? No. The good ones are the ones who reach inside and find a way to bring out their best, day in and day out. When they asked Joe DiMaggio why he played every game like the pennant depended on it, he answered, "Did you see those 60,000 fans? One of them might be a kid seeing me play for the first time."

Story time! I was in a stage production of *Vanities* in Canada. From the get-go, it was obvious to me that the director was in over his head. As soon as he got off the plane, he said, "This play is all about women and I know nothing about them. I don't understand them."

Okay. Fine. We have one week of rehearsal before curtain. Now what? Actually, that wasn't the question. The question was "What can I do about this?"

So, I called in a very good friend, a fabulous director in Texas.

Would he come and help? "I need you." He also was a fabulous costume designer (fabulous squared!). The so-called director had made no provisions for our cheerleader outfits. He thought they didn't have cheerleaders in Canada. They didn't. We certainly needed those costumes. The story described the lives of three women, beginning as cheerleaders in high school and ending with ten years after college.

My friend from Texas was Larry Randolph. Our arrangement was our secret. During the day, while we rehearsed with the original director, Larry constructed our cheerleader outfits on the bed of my apartment with a portable sewing machine. At night, we moved the furniture around. The cast came to my apartment and Larry blocked (that's stage lingo for positioning actors on stage and then telling them where to move) and directed the play.

The original director never knew. We would come in the next day with the scene working beautifully because of the last night's rehearsal and the director would say, "That's great, girls."

Why all this trouble? Because I knew my name was on the billboard. Patrons paid to see me in a good production. What if, like Joe DiMaggio, they were seeing me for the first time? I'm not a diva, but if I am in a bad production, the show isn't a failure, I am.

We completed the show and got great reviews and the director never knew. Larry Randolph and I worked together many times before and since. He is just fabulous. He never got any credit for that show. That's a true friend.

It's my job.

When I'm in a stage production, I know many in the audience come to see what Mary Ann looks like. They want to size up how I look compared to the Mary Ann of the past. My job is to make them leave the theater with a new experience with Dawn Wells.

It needs to be an experience that is new and exceptional. *Pause button here.* Sometimes the billboards say, "Live! On Stage!" It makes me laugh. I can't help thinking about the alternative — dead on stage. *Pause button off.*

That's why I am so particular about the plays I choose to do. If they came to see Mary Ann, I want them to leave glad that they saw Dawn Wells. It's often a TV audience coming to see me, and for some, it is their first theater experience. My goal is to create a new theater-goer.

And sometimes it's like I'm in a zoo. Hey! Throw me a peanut! Come see me *live!*

Think of yourself as a business.

Step outside yourself and look at yourself in the way you would regard a business. *Voila!* You aren't *you* anymore. You are Myself, Inc. Hmmm. Where to begin?

What is the company image?
How is it seen out there in the world?
What is your logo?
What is your mission statement?

What is it like to do business with Myself, Inc.?
What is your business plan?
When is the last time you updated the plan?

You are the president, chief executive officer, chief financial officer, maintenance department, advertising director, production department and chief cook and bottle washer at Myself, Inc. You can't pass the buck. Well, you can, but you'll be passing it to yourself. You are in charge and you are *solely* responsible for the performance of the company.

Think about that one. You hear people say "Everything happens for a reason." Well, now the reason is you. Maybe things are happening to you — or not happening to you — because you aren't managing Myself, Inc., properly.

Roadwork ahead!

Here are Mary Ann's Signposts on the Road to Special:

Know your brand.
You hear that word a lot lately. Your "brand." Let's think of it another way. Let's call it your "aura." Ooh, how New Age! Okay, what is it?

What are your corporate colors? Are you institutional deep blues and steel grays? Are you satiny pastels? Are you hot-blooded primary colors? There is no wrong answer here, unless you are a hot-blooded primary in an institutional color scheme — or vice versa. That can get dicey.

Does your company font match your color? (We are designing your logo, here, if you haven't noticed.) Are you trying to match an authoritative font with a wild red? Might work. With a soft pastel pink or yellow? Hmmm.

What does your brand, your aura, say about you?
Are you competent, creative, and credentialed?
Or are you timid, so-so, and sluggish?
Are you forceful or laid back or in between?
Are you driven or are you "okay with it"?

I could go on — I'm making this up as I go, you know — but you get the idea.

Who *are* you? Does the who you *are* match the who you *present* to the world? Wait, that's not the question. Try this: *Is the who you present to the world the who you want to be?*

Show up.
You wouldn't think this to be a tough one. Wrongo! I have seen so many talented people fade from entertainment careers because they simply weren't dependable. It never ceases to amaze me. I mean, you can't do the job if you aren't there. Think what kind of business Myself, Inc., would do if the shop closed on a whim.

Prepare.
You also can't do the job if you aren't ready. *Showing up doesn't mean just being there.* In show business it means knowing your script, understanding your character, hitting your marks. It's prepare, prepare, prepare. At Myself, Inc., it means . . . what? If Myself, Inc., has the equivalent of a noon rush, or a big sale, or a

JIM BACKUS AND "GOLDEN TIME"

Jim Backus was very sweet and fun, but he was also very much Thurston Howell III. He was wealthy and notoriously cheap.

Jim would invite Natalie Schafer and me to nice lunches and invariably arrive conveniently having "forgotten" his wallet. After the first year of this, Natalie presented him with a bill. "Jim, you owe us $386 for lunch." I don't know if he ever paid it. Jim called me "The Go-To Girl." Why? Because I knew most of the Screen Actors Guild rules. On long days, overtime would sometimes extend into "Golden Time." Our salaries really went sky high in Golden Time. Jim would ask me if we were nearing Golden Time. If I said yes, he would suddenly need to visit the restroom. When he reappeared, Golden Time would have kicked in.

He really was Mr. Howell, wasn't he? A lovely man. Adorable . . . and he got me a lot of Golden Time, too. He shared his comedic talent and timing openly, always advising and always wanting to help us all. His generosity with himself was sweet.

critical presentation, then the staff (a.k.a. *you*) needs to be poised and ready.

Story time! I was once invited to make "the gorilla climb" in Rwanda. What's that? Well, you climb the mountains to view the mountain gorillas in their natural habitat. These giant, gentle creatures are nearly extinct because of poaching.

Very few women have made this climb. It is a once-in-a-lifetime adventure. I was with incredible women. For me, it would be exceedingly difficult because, as you know by now, my knees dislocate.

Well, I wanted to be ready! I started training for the climb. I started by working out in a pool. It wasn't long before my knees began to swell. I went to my doctor, and bless Doc Kagan's heart. He said I should stop training because I could damage my knees so much I might not make the climb at all. If I make it up the mountain and my knees swell, then somebody will carry me down.

Halfway up the mountain, one of the other climbers complained he was having knee trouble. He asked to borrow my knee supports. He put them on and immediately descended the mountain. The cad! There I was with no knee guards and half a mountain to climb. I made it to the top! It was wonderful. There we were among the gorillas, an arm's length away. It was a glorious, awesome experience.

And, yes, some of our guides carried me part of the way back down. Normally, they balanced the group's large packs and coolers atop their heads. They didn't carry me that way, thank heaven.

When we got to the bottom of the mountain I gave them half of my clothes in appreciation. Hmmm, did that make me "half naked"?

Return calls.
Return everything. There are so many different ways to communicate now. Use them all. The people you work with and the people you want to work with will have a favorite method. They may prefer email over phone, or text message over email. Whatever. Some industries have preferred communication styles. Some industries still use fax machines. If you have a working relationship with people, find out their preferences and communicate their way.

Here is Mary Ann's rule of thumb: Return any communication within that business day. Nobody knows what you are thinking until you tell them. Duh. So, tell them. Don't sit on a message. Don't let it grow cold. Stay in their information flow. The people you work with will appreciate this, even if they don't do it themselves.

You know when you call a business and the message says, "You're call is very important to us." At Myself, Inc., make that your motto. While you are at it,

Keep the formality.
Don't get too casual just because it's a text or email instead of a letter. Don't force the person on the other end to fill in the blanks on your messages. Think them through. Slow down. Write them well.

Do what you say will do.

Well, duh, again! How hard can this one be? Well, if my experience is a measure, it is very, very difficult. It happens all the time.

You need someone to do such and such.
You ask a person if he *can do* such and such.
The person says yes.
You ask the person if he *wants to do* such and such.
He says yes.
You ask the person if he can do such and such *today*.
He says yes.
The day goes by. No such and such.
You call.
He answers: "Oh, yeah! Such and such! Workin' on it!"
The next day passes. No such and such.
You call.
He answers: "Oh, yeah! Such and such! Wrappin' it up now!"
That day passes. No such and such.
On the third day you call.
He doesn't answer.

You dance the No Answer Two Step with him for a day, maybe two. It all fades to gray. You call another person. Can he do such and such? Yes…and you go into the same cycle.

It makes you want to scream. "Why the *such and such* can't I get a such and such!!!!" Ooh, four exclamation points.

Myself, Inc., always comes through. Myself, Inc., always delivers. You can depend on Myself, Inc. That's the brand. (By the way, the unofficial motto of Canada's Royal Canadian Mounted Police is

"We always get our man." I don't know if Myself, Inc., wants to adopt that motto, but hey, I thought I'd throw it at you.)

Claiming you can do something you cannot do is an unmistakable sign that your little brain is in charge of that moment. Failing to follow through on a task you accepted is a sign that your little brain is in charge of your life. These may be the two things which most clearly separate the good ones from the average ones. Which brings me to…

Never accept mediocrity.
Ugh. Mediocrity. Average. Pedestrian. Another flavor of vanilla. Mediocrity is seductive. It's so easy. It can seem so easy to hide — mediocrity puts you into a pack with most of the others. It's *adequate*. It's not like the job didn't get done at all.

Runners sometimes train by weighing themselves down. They strap weights on their arms and legs. They even wear weighted vests. Accepting mediocrity is like strapping on those weights. It's a drag on you. Like the runners, if you remove those weights just watch how far and fast you can go.

Sometimes mediocrity results from an illusion. You think you *are* doing fine. You think, "Hey, I'm still here. I'm getting a paycheck." Okay. How do you know?

Time to call in the Big Brain.

Better yet, let's call in the board of directors of Myself, Inc. Let's have a performance evaluation! The Myself, Inc., board of directors and the president, CEO, CFO, maintenance department, advertising director, production department, and chief cook and bottle washer at Myself, Inc., and have an honest analysis.

Rising above mediocrity requires honesty. You must be honest with yourself. "Can I do better? How? Why not?"

At Myself, Inc., you understand that mediocrity is the path toward going out of business. It's only a matter of time before a better business comes along and takes your customers away.

There is no middle of the road for Myself, Inc., on the Road to Special. There is no run of the mill challenge that is genuinely a challenge. You must be the best and know you are.

Be an adult.
Myself, Inc., isn't a lemonade stand. It is a full-blown business. Okay, so maybe it's a startup. Doesn't matter. You are on the stage of life. You are on the Road to Special. Act like you belong there. No company can last long with an immature president.

Know what you want.
You can't make good decisions if you don't. Being strong doesn't mean you can't be feminine.

Story time! Barbara Eden is a wonderful example. I worked with her in one of my very first productions — a movie called *The New Interns* directed by John Rich. It had quite a cast — Barbara, Greg Morris, Telly Savalas, Stefanie Powers, Michael Callan, Dean Jones . . . and moi.

Barbara and I became fast friends. I learned from her. She is everything you see on camera. Very sweet and feminine. But I also saw a strong side. She has a business head and knows where to draw lines. Why? Barbara always knows what she wants. Still, she never lost her femininity. Her sense of humor. She had great advice. She is a woman I respect in every area.

A little side note here: I never cried with a director. Crying is for children. I'm talking about anger and tears. Hurt feelings and tears. Frustration and tears. I'm not talking tears of joy or sentiment. Hey, I tear up at *the commercials* during the holidays, for heaven's sake. Dawn Wells can be reduced to sobs from the seat of any theater. Dawn Wells, Inc. *never* cries. I see so many actresses who use tears to get what they want. If you are adult enough for the position, you are adult enough to handle rejection and criticism.

Never stop.
I have never considered retirement. I've watched too many people wither away after they removed work from their lives. At the same time, I know that retirement works for many people, and I applaud that. I'm just not one of them. I'll never retire.

I'm talking about growing. Never stop growing. Businesses must grow in order to stay in business. The same is true of Myself, Inc. How does Myself, Inc., grow? Just like a business. You establish a plan and you follow the plan as best you can.

Maybe you just make constant improvement part of your "corporate culture." What does constant improvement mean? You can learn more.

You can tackle new tasks. You can develop a new skill. You can get better at the skills you have.

Learn a new language.
Learn a new skill.
Adopt a new hobby.
Tackle a new task.

Can't you just feel your Big Brain swinging into action just thinking about it?

Enjoy the small print.
At Myself, Inc., we don't let things pile up our desk. You know what I'm talking about – The Things We Must Do That Are Not Much Fun. In my experience, these are what I call the Small Print of Life.

They are the Gotta Do's. It's the driver's license renewals, the insurance forms, the termite inspections, and remembering to get that spare house key made. It's reseeding the lawn, updating your résumé, and staying in touch. *It's having a To-Do list and making it To-Done.*

When you think about it, the Gotta Do's make up most of our lives. Have you ever painted something? No, I don't mean a landscape. I mean, say, the walls of your room. When the idea first comes, it's so easy to picture yourself, contented, rolling paint on the wall and making everything all new. Yet, very little of the total package of time is spent actually laying paint to surface.

No. It's moving furniture around and away, it's the masking and sanding and cleaning and placing the drop cloth and assembling the tools and stirring the paint. Not to mention picking the colors and buying the paint. Oh, and you have to clean the tools, store the leftover paint and rearrange the room when you are done.

You will enrich life all the more — and Myself, Inc., will perform better — if you can find a way to enjoy the Gotta Do's. I mean, really, do you want that much of your life to be deemed a nuisance? Funny, isn't it, you have to engage your Big Brain to get the Gotta Do's done? Accomplishment gives you sense of confidence.

Mind the books.
Remember, you are the chief financial officer (CFO) of Myself, Inc. The CFO makes budgets and strives to stay within them. The CFO knows how to balance a checkbook. The CFO has one credit card and pays it monthly. The CFO knows exactly how much money Myself, Inc., has at any given time. It's not much more complicated than that.

Everybody, *everybody* is emotional about money. The emotions money triggers in you are personal and unique to you. The emotions other people carry are unlike yours. Look, we've all got that pair of shoes in the closet we never should have bought. We all just arrived at the purchase decision in different ways.

If you can truly analyze yourself, if you can truly be self-aware enough, if you can turn emotional decisions into rational decisions, you will put Myself, Inc., in a better position to grow.

I've done okay for myself. I've never been taken care of other than as a child. I learned very early to read all my contracts and to learn as much about finance as I could. I often wished I had more training.

Just because you earned a lot of money doesn't mean you will keep it. Learning finance is as important as learning how to brush your teeth.

And this, friends, is the joy of working.

Work gives you a feeling of accomplishment. A job completed, a job well done, opens doors. It leads to more jobs. Work should be a pleasure for you. There should be pleasure in the doing and joy in the completion.

I have never envied people who lead lives of leisure. *Our work defines us.* It is one of the things that gives us meaning. Work unites us. It puts us in relationships based on need and trust and accountability.

MARY ANN'S TERRIBLE TOO'S

Too uninspired
Too ordinary
Too indolent
Too slack
Too slipshod
Too unreliable
Too whiny
Too dicey
Too lax
Too late, too often

Illustration by James Bennett

entertainer

act • ing

noun

: the art or profession of performing the role of a character in a play, movie, etc.
: the art or profession of an actor

artist
thespian
TROUPER

PERFORMER

PLAYER

STAR

So, you want to be in show business

Acting is not about being someone different. It's finding the similarity in what is apparently different, then finding myself in there.
— Meryl Streep

The reason they call it show business is because it is a business. If you want to be in the business, treat it like a business.

I have mentored many, many young people who wanted to be in show business. Wait. Let's amend that. Young people who *thought* they wanted to be in show business. I often meet the kids I mentor through my alma mater, Stephens College. For many years, I had a small guest house. The kids would stay there while they tried out Hollywood. I want to tell three stories that more or less sum up my experience as a mentor.

Story one. She came. She stayed.

The first was a young woman who wanted to become a screenwriter. She arrived with a single-mindedness (is that a word?) that was palpable. She worked on her craft. She met people. She learned the industry. She got a job that started her career as a writer. She's still at it.

Story two. He came. He tried.

The second was a young man, a dancer. I saw him dance and I

wanted to meet him. Even then, he had his own style. We talked. He told me his dream was to be a dancer. I told him, "You have to go where the work is. You have your own style. The time line is slim." I invited him to come to Los Angeles. I met his family. He came and stayed about three years.

He focused on career development from the beginning. He trained hard and found work as an actor and as a dancer in music videos. In the end, it wasn't enough. He wanted more from life. That's why he returned to his hometown. He is now a fabulous teacher at a junior high school. He got Hollywood out of his system. He could have stayed and worked in show business, but he knew who he was. He's doing what he wants to do now and we have remained good friends. He has a wonderful family.

Story three. She came. She quit.

The third story is a young woman who also stayed with me. She worked for me, got a job with a caterer and eventually got a job as a bartender. When I asked her what acting classes she was taking, she said she didn't have the money for classes. I said, "You have to have the money."

I tried to explain to her that being part of classes and workshops reach far beyond just learning how to act. She could meet people. Actors help each other. Actors clue each other in on auditions and available roles. They share information and introduce each other to opportunities. She needed to be where that was happening.

And then the day came when I told her she was putting on a little too much weight. It hurt her feelings. I told her it wasn't a matter of how she felt, it was a matter of how she looked. In the end, she quit and went home.

These are typical stories. Notice that the first story is the simplest to tell.

If you get into acting with the sole purpose of being a star, you won't be a star. Period. If that is what you are here for, you are wasting your time.

Charisma makes stars.
It's a connection with the audience, talent notwithstanding. There are a million people with a million talents who aren't stars. You cannot make stardom happen, but you must be prepared if it does. Don't expect it. Love your work. Stardom is a bonus.

To be a star, you must first be a working actor.
You must earn a living doing the craft you love. You don't decide to be a lawyer because you look good in a three-piece suit.

Acting — show business — is hard work and long hours.
Sure, you hear about the parties. Those who are really working don't have much time for them.

It has to be real.
"Personalities" are not actors. Pretending is not acting (think reality shows here). Beauty comes and goes. Sex symbols fade.

Actors must be knowledgeable.
You need to know history, language, current events . . . how

things work. If you are playing a character in World War II, you need to know about World War II. If you are going to play Shakespeare, you need to know Shakespeare.

Actors never stop working.
If you aren't working, you should be in a class or a workshop. Reading. Rehearsing. Attending to the physical you.

If you aren't training, you are losing "acting muscle." The world around you is a workshop. There are behaviors to observe and vocal accents to gather.

Good actors never stop honing their craft.
While we were shooting *Gilligan's Island*, I was taking classes in acting. I studied. I participated in workshops. I took voice lessons. I learned it all — building sets, stage managing, wardrobe, applying makeup, and on and on — at Stephens College and the University of Washington.

Show business geography is shifting.
The entertainment world is much bigger and more varied than the day I auditioned for *Gilligan's Island*. There are more opportunities. You aren't limited to New York and Los Angeles. Movies and shows are being made outside these two markets and are being made with fewer rules. Think of the internet alone. Many are non-union.

Show business opportunities are growing.
What a list! Infomercials, industrials, voiceovers, hosting, regional theater, summer stock, internet.

Find your niche.

John Wayne never made a musical. Jack Benny never played a cowboy. If you look like a cowboy, then train yourself to walk and talk like a cowboy. If have a Mediterranean look, then learn vocal accents that will let you cross over multiple nationalities — from Italy to the Middle East.

This is a conundrum for many young people. "Can I be all things or just one thing?" Be realistic and self critical about what you really look like, your type. During casting, when you walk in the door, you are either right or wrong. If you are physically nondescript, you probably have more opportunity for work than if you are extremely "typed."

Perhaps I got the Mary Ann role instead of Raquel Welch because I looked more the type. Maybe it's no more complicated than that.

I am always aware of the qualifications and the job. I know where I stand on a talent scale of 1 to 10. I know what my physical attributes are. I know what I can do.

Now, break the mold.

Once you are typecast, what does it mean? Well, it means you will spend the majority of your career in a narrow slot or it means you can change as you age and improve along the way, gradually and with foresight. You may be able to work all the time. You may have the ability to create a whole new professional persona. Knock their socks off doing the role no one expects.

I stopped mentioning that I was Miss Nevada after a few weeks in Hollywood. I needed to be more than a beauty queen. I had a meeting with Jack Warner. We talked. Afterwards, he remarked to my agent that we had engaged in an actual *conversation*. By that he meant we talked about topics other than business. Most important, we talked about topics other than ourselves.

Here's the point: If there is so much more to Dawn Wells than people think they know, it is up to me to show it. Nobody is going to go to the trouble to find that out on their own. I had to be careful not to make the mold I would later have to break.

As soon as the *Gilligan's Island* series ended, I knew that as Mary Ann matured I had to break that mold. I did not stay in television because it would be more typecasting. My first job after *Gilligan's Island* was playing a hooker in a stage production of *The Owl and the Pussycat*.

From there on I followed the paths that took me further from Mary Ann. Hey, she was already right there in your living room, year in and year out. Why add more? At the same time, I couldn't help throwing a little Mary Ann into the hooker character. I gave her a heart of gold. I grew. I improved. I stretched.

How many *Barefoot in the Park* productions could I have done? The answer is: Too many. I want each role to be a stretch. Nobody could believe it when I did *Man-in-the-Moon Marigolds* or *Lion in Winter*. But I am grateful to have fit a "type." I worked and learned and was ready for the next step. Growth and challenges. I didn't want to keep on playing the Mary Ann character.

I'LL TRY ANYTHING

Make that *almost* anything. I did my first musical at age 40.

There was a problem: I really can't sing. I have a long history of bad singing. I was gently removed from the children's choir at my church when I was in the sixth grade. It wasn't for behavioral reasons. I was asked to teach Sunday School instead.

On the set during an episode of *Gilligan's Island,* Sherwood asked me to mouth the words while we were singing "For He's a Jolly Good Fellow." Yes, I was off-key.

In the movie *Winter Hawk*, I played a missionary, and in one scene, I was supposed to lead a group song of "Amazing Grace." After a few false starts, the director put a girl under my long skirt. She sang the song. I mouthed the words.

I took some singing lessons from Phoebe Binkley, a fabulous voice teacher in Nashville. She said, "You aren't tone deaf. You just don't have any musical memory."

The best response, though, came during an audition for a stage production of *They're Playing our Song*. The producer stopped me mid-song and said, "This is a musical, isn't it?"

I did part of the national tour. It nearly killed me.

I've embraced Mary Ann my whole life. But, what could I do with Mary Ann? I couldn't just keep on playing that character.

Show business is demanding.

Show business can fool you. The whole idea is to make it look easy. That guy juggling five balls, ooh, he looks so nonchalant. He will never reveal the hours of effort it took to make it look effortless.

An acting career is one of long days, often in some discomfort. It is one of predawn preparation and late evening review.

I've read that it takes 10,000 hours of practice — that's around three hours a day for ten years — to become truly accomplished at something. This can be true of that juggler or a pianist or painter or a singer or surgeon. I believe that 10,000 number is true.

You have to work at being an actor. Actors who show up unprepared don't last long. Actors who don't take their roles seriously — and sometimes the silliest roles require the most serious development — often find themselves replaced.

There are deadlines to meet. It is hardly different from a manufacturing business. You are, after all, part of a team that is making a product that must be delivered on time. There are contracts to read. You need to read them yourself. Read them slowly. Take the time to understand them. Sure, you'll need a lawyer, but never sign a document you have not read!!! (That's three exclamation points, but it really means four. No. Make that six.)

Stage vs. screen.

Being funny without an audience is *very* difficult. When we shot *Gilligan's Island*, there were no studio audiences. Today it's the norm to have one. What a difference!

I still marvel at Bob Denver and his comic timing . . . without an audience. How long to hold for the laugh? How long to hold for the kiss? When it's live, on stage, audiences will react and signal you. You can feel it.

On stage you have to rely on instinct. You are doing a real dramatic scene. You have to walk across a stage and get a vase and throw it through a window. Halfway across the stage you realize there is no vase there. Now you have to make it work. Your mind and your body and your mouth are performing and rewriting the moment at the same time.

In film you can just forget it. No, that's not right. You may be able to recreate moments. However, there are also crucial moments on camera that pass and cannot be recreated. It's a very different craft. Preparing the character is the same. One of the things they say to you is "Can you act on camera?" Can you be as subtle for the camera as you are broad for the stage?

Show business people are people.

They respond to the same things — courtesy, integrity, promptness . . . thank you notes! Look, if you are competing for a part and it's a three-or four-way tie talentwise (which happens more often than you might think), who do you think the director is going to choose? Little Miss Pouty over there? Try to understand the people you deal with. Remember that a casting director probably wanted to be an actor at one time. Control your emotions. Artists are emotional people, by and large. Emotions are not useful in a business environment. The same characteristics that will make you preferred in other fields will work in show business. Your character is as important as your talent.

Show business requires optimism.

Remember Babe Ruth and his strikeouts? You could wind up with almost that many in show business. Auditions are hard. Rejection is the norm. The same goes for writers and producers. You are only as good as your last hit. If a picture bombs, it just gets that much harder to get backing for your next one.

There are other jobs in the business.

It isn't just all in front of the camera. There is the business of making and producing films. If you are interested in show business there are other jobs connected to the business off the stage or behind the camera. There are lot of ways to get a job and a lot of jobs to get — makeup, hair, casting, script supervision, and on and on and on. Just watch the credits roll on a movie or television show. Learn all the other areas in the businesses. There are so many essential areas of the industry. You can find a place to fit.

The casting couch.

The "casting couch" — the exchange of sexual favors for a role — is largely a myth. I have never encountered it. A casting director's job is on the line, just like everybody else's. The casting director gets you in front of the writer and the producer and director. You are on a list of possibilities. A casting couch decision would be a big risk on a $20 million picture. Everybody's job is on the line.

Try it and give yourself time.

A *Gilligan's Island* work week.

We produced one episode per week on the set of *Gilligan's Island*. It was a five-day week. They were long days. We often arrived for work in the dark and left in the dark. In the beginning, Mondays started with a table read of that week's script (it was delivered to the cast on the weekend before. It was left on my porch.) However, table reads were eliminated because there was too much physical comedy that just didn't come across in a table read.

We shot for a week. The script would change as the week progressed. Each edition of edited pages came in on different colored paper. We often had as many as five or six different colors.

I had the early call for makeup. I was low man on the totem pole, so to speak, so I was first in at 6 a.m. I was usually up at 4 a.m. to make the call. It was hair first, then makeup, then body makeup. It took about an hour and a half. Then it was off to the dressing room.

The outdoor shots for *Gilligan's Island* took place at the "lagoon" one or two days a week. The lagoon was built on a lot near our sound stage after it proved too foggy to shoot in nearby Malibu. (As I remember, they always managed to put me in that lagoon in

January.) The rest of the week was shot indoors. We had the huts in Sound Stage 2.

We used real plants on the sets. They were all in pots and were maintained by "greens men."

Later in the week, the lagoon was turned into a lake for *Gunsmoke*. The palm trees and tropical plants were replaced with tumbleweeds and sage brush. It's one thing to rearrange the furniture. It is another to rearrange the landscape. That always fascinated me.

Ah, the lagoon. It's gone now. They cemented over it last year. It's a parking lot. I guess that's progress.

We shot like a movie. The director was on set. Today, the director would be in a booth watching a screen. There is a lot of downtime on a set. Hurry up and wait. Always be ready. At noon, the network executives would show up and go to the screening room to review the "rushes" – the film shot the day before. Today, those are instantly available. I watched the rushes, too. I was the only cast member allowed to watch them. Why? I was objective.

Most directors don't want actors to see the "dailies." They might want to change their performances when the director already liked what he saw. I analyzed my work without emotion. I considered that a huge asset for my future performance. I didn't use the opportunity to request changes from the director. For me, it was a learning experience for the art of performance and for my physical image.

We all worked long days, but Bob Denver invariably worked the longest. Bobby did a lot of his own stunts, along with his stunt double, Bobby d'Arcy.

We usually wrapped on Friday evening. Our craft service guy, Angelo, would produce fantastic food on the craft service tables, perhaps his famous lasagna. The crew brought wine and we had a little party. Here's a surprise. Quite often, Thurston actually sprang for the wine.

What might have been . . . And the rest

In retrospect, the key to the success of *Gilligan's Island* was the casting, but oh, how different it could have been.

It was rumored that Sherwood Schwartz wanted to cast Carroll O'Connor as Thurston Howell III and he offered Jerry Van Dyke the role of Gilligan. Russell Johnson was the second choice for the role of the Professor. After Jim Backus was cast as Mr. Howell, I think his wife wanted the part of…his wife. Natalie Schafer got it.

I believe Sherwood's brother created the role of Ginger. In the pilot episode, there were three teachers.

More than 300 women auditioned for the role of Mary Ann, including Raquel Welch and just about every ingénue in town. It took a week. The roles were altered after the pilot episode. When CBS bought the show, they wanted a rewrite. The writers created three new characters — a movie star, a professor, and a farm girl. The Mary Ann character was originally a teacher named "Bunny." She was re-written as a farm girl from Winfield, Kansas.

Meanwhile, the Ginger character moved from being a teacher to a movie star. Because of the cast changes, the pilot wasn't shown when the series began.

Sherwood Schwartz wanted the theme song of the show to summarize the premise of the show – who we were, how we got there and what we needed to do. CBS also wanted the song to explain our predicament. This was the first time (at least I think so. I don't want to look it up).

The original song described the roles of Gilligan, The Skipper, The Howells, and the movie star, but did not describe the Professor or Mary Ann, who were referred to as "the rest." This created one of the questions most asked about the show. Why were they "the rest"?

I was told the reason was this. Ginger was cast first on the East Coast before the Professor and Mary Ann were cast on the West Coast.

Ginger's agent negotiated that she was in fifth position billing. She followed the Howells and nobody would come after her. Russell and I then became "The Rest." Up until Russell's death, we sent each other cards signed, "Love, The Rest".

While writing this, we lost my dear Professor. We were "The Rest" and he was "The Best." I dearly loved Russell. He was always a gentleman. A great actor. He had an unequaled sense of humor. He was truly the funniest of all of us. He was my dear friend and will be missed.

The theme song changed the second season. We got our billing. Three people were credited for this — Bob Denver, Sherwood Schwartz and John Rich, our director. I don't know who it was, but thank you.

Love, The Rest

MARY ANN'S TERRIBLE TOO'S

Too unprofessional

Too incompetent

Too negligent

Too unprepared

Too temperamental

Too demanding

Too self involved

Too impolite

Too tardy

Too unfocused

Illustration by James Bennett

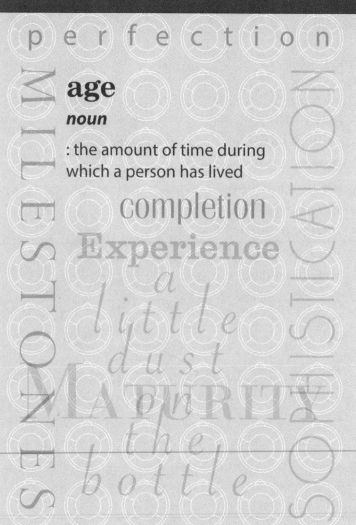

perfection

age
noun

: the amount of time during
which a person has lived

completion

Experience

a little dust on the bottle

MILESTONES

SOPHISTICATION

MATURITY

Hey! Who's that old gal in the mirror?

The afternoon knows what the morning never suspected.

— Robert Frost

Natalie Schafer had seventeen Broadway plays on her résumé before she forever became Lovey Howell on *Gilligan's Island*. She was a guest star on many television series before and after *Gilligan's Island*. In the movies, she often played The Other Woman.

She was rich and famous and fresh from starring in *Gilligan's Island* and "old enough to be your mother" when a young pup television executive at ABC brought her in for an interview. The suit sits her down in his Manhattan office. "Now," he asks her, "What have you done?"

Natalie looks him over, raising her lorgnette, and says, "You first."

They are still talking about that in Los Angeles today.

I loved Natalie and still love her today. We became very close friends after the show. We spent a lot time together in California and New York and Florida. I want to live to be a hundred. Natalie almost made it.

I've said it before. Age is a pre-existing condition.

So deal with it. Make it work for you. I can't believe how old I am. So many trips around the sun as I write this. I'm grateful. I want to be Betty White when I grow up.

I have always looked forward and don't ever want to stop. I will always ask, "Am I the best that I can be?" Age has nothing to do with the question. Or everything. Age tells you what best is. It strips away the illusions. Lets you say, "You first."

I am happy to be on the planet, I am happy to be alive.

My age fascinates me. If the old saying is true — "You are as old as you think" — then I don't know how old I am. If you ask me, I guess I'll just hold up all my fingers and smile. Age is a state of mind. Late in life, my mother, all five feet and 90 pounds of her, was walking with me in a shopping mall. She saw her reflection in a shop window. She started looking around, wondering who that old lady was.

The Things I Want to Do make for a long list. I want to see Antarctica. I want to see the ocean depths. I want to learn how to paint. Maybe I'll decamp to an elder hostel to learn . . . something. Horse camp! I'll finally ride English saddle. Study another language. Ballroom dancing. Italy for a cooking class. Falling in love again. I still haven't done Broadway!

I don't think you can live every minute when you are young. You aren't aware of just how many minutes you get. You can look at age as making a new friend. It makes your life bigger. It's the other side. A friend of mine announced at age 65 that she was gay. It took her awhile, but she got there.

In show business you are always made aware of what is age appropriate. The business takes care of that for you. You don't get to decide if you are still an ingénue, show business does. If you stick with show business you watch your roles change as you age.

This means you get to come into your own again and again and again. Each new age bracket brings new roles, new challenges. Your skills are polished until they gleam. In theater, they always say the real tragedy of *Hamlet* is that by time you are a good enough actor to play him, you are too old.

There are countless women over 60 who are still getting it done. (By the way, Natalie swam naked in her pool every day until she died at 91.)

Age gives you a different take on culture. You know how the culture got here. You watched it. You lived it. At my age, you no longer live in the culture you made. Well, you made it, and then you watched as the next generations unmade it. From my age, it isn't that hard to tell what was made better and what was made worse. Cue the grumpy old broad swatting children away with her cane!

Oh, but things have changed.

We live longer. Much longer. We are healthier. We are more fit. We look better. Somebody, somewhere, is constantly telling us that age 60 is the new . . . whatever — the numbers keep changing. Technology keeps us young, connected to each other and to youth.

Plastic surgery has evolved from a Hollywood secret to an out-patient day trip. What sags gets lifted. What wrinkles gets stretched. What is too small is made large. What is too large is shrunk.

Music crosses generations. You don't have to poke in some dusty back-bin to find your favorite music on out-of-print albums. There it is, digitally remastered and ready for download. Just like it's brand new.

How many relationships can you have in a very long, very full life? How many do you need? How many do you want?

And that, ladies, is the problem. I don't pretend to know why people get divorced. I only know why I did. It's just too personal. I do know, though, that we live longer and I don't have to look around much to see a crowd of older women standing over there in the singles section. It's a restless crowd. I think that's because there are too many directions to choose and none of them looks just right.

My older single credentials: I've been single since 1967 and that's the way I've wanted it. I know what I'm talking about here, ladies.

So, to simplify this little exercise, let's use ages 25, 50 and 75. Just pick the one that closest applies to you.

The last thing you want to do is to play 25 when you are 50. Play by your own rules. Fifty is freedom. Your ego isn't on the line anymore. You know who you are. Maybe you've stepped off the Road to Special for a while, but you know how to get back on.

When you play by your own rules, you can use the "L" word. You can act like a Lady and expect to be treated like one. It doesn't matter what the 25-year olds are doing. You're 50. You don't care what they think. Open the door for me. Hold me on your arm. Walk with me on the correct side. Take my coat.

It's not about mating anymore. You aren't looking for a father for your children. It's about friendship, connection and common interest and physical attraction. And fun!

This is so great. Why are you so serious? Every date isn't an audition for a lifetime commitment. It's just two, maybe three hours of companionship. Dinner and a slow dance, done. Ball game and a hotdog, done. You can look for someone who broadens you, stimulates you, enhances you. Everyone has a story. Go out with him and hear it. We might actually learn something.

Thank heavens they invented coffee shops. It's a bar without the stupid.

I've never dated men in show business. It's all about them. It just never seems to work. Way too much little brain in the mix. When I was 25 I wanted a mover and a shaker. (Do they still say that?) He needed to be sharp. (Do they still say that?) A man who other men admire. (I know they still say *that*.) I don't want or need that so much in a man anymore. Now, I want to see what a man offers as a human being.

Try expecting this from a man and see what happens:

A sense of humor.
A positive outlook.
A kind spirit.
A polite person.
A good man.
A good father.
A good sport.
A good partner.
Someone who stimulates my brain.
Someone who isn't shallow.

Make that men. When you are just dating, you can have a lot of men in your life, especially if you are 50 or 75. I do. You might find that one man isn't enough. It has nothing to do with a sexual partner. You may have too many interests. Me, I always want to hear more stories. I want to be with men who take my mind to new places. Fascinate me. Engage my Big Brain!

I have many male friends. I have a friend who travels constantly. When he's in town we go to dinner. It's a lovely evening. He is a Renaissance Man. (Do they still say that?) Nothing escapes his curiosity. I can feel my Big Brain responding to him, but that's all. It's a dinner and that's it.

I have another friend, a Marine, who may show up where I am when I travel. We go out to dinner. Different man, different portion of my Big Brain. What do they all have in common? They are not romantic entanglements.

SHE NEVER PLAYED HER AGE

Natalie Schafer never revealed her age.

It was written into her contract that there would be no close-up shots of her in *Gilligan's Island*. Somehow word leaked that her year of birth was 1912.

What a life. She used to tell of hijinks with her friends from the New York theater circle.

Risque charades or being "kidnapped" and taken to Cape Cod.

I wonder how old we were here.
Photo: Dawn Wells Archives

She was wealthy. High Society. Rodeo Drive and Park Avenue. When she wasn't dressed and glamorous, which was almost always, she was in her pool swimming naked. She dreaded the idea of becoming a "hausfrau'" or an old lady in a bathrobe.

Just before her house sold, I asked her manager if I could have the rose bushes. They are still blooming. I recently moved and took them with me. It's a very special memory.

I discovered recently she was born in 1900.

I have a another friend who is very dapper. (Do they still say that?) He is great arm candy and a companion for events. He's fun. We are friends. I think that comes with a certain age.

And now, I have a special man who has my heart. He touches my soul, my mind, my being. Here I am, and it's only the beginning. We'll see.

Not a love affair. Something in common.

If you are 50 and single, it isn't the end of the Road to Special. It's not even a rest stop. Do new things. Do the same things you've always done in a different way. If you hear yourself saying, "I don't think I'd like that," ask yourself, "How do you know?" I'm still discovering like I was 25.

You are older. You can pick and choose. The more full you are as a person, the more exciting you will be as a companion. You emit a new kind of magnetism. Fascinate him. Electrify his Big Brain.

First, of course, you have to find them. I don't know how much help I can be here. Hmmm. Let's see. Men make up half the population. They are in grocery stores, at sports events, art museums, gyms, and churches. They belong to book clubs and bicycle clubs. They volunteer. They play bridge. They…oh you get the point. Be friends first. Find something in common. Something may develop or not.

It's up to you to get out of the house. If you insist on being the old broad in a bathrobe, well, enjoy the daytime television.

Oops. Found one.

Just when think you are in full dating mode, something starts telling you that a man and a woman together make a better human being. You see it. The contentment. He pushes the cart. She picks the groceries. A team. There is a certain unspoken wisdom in it all.

In the stage play *Children of Eden*, the actor in the role of God sings, "What good is having a universe if you have no one to give it to?" Then, he creates Adam. I've never heard it put better. Yes, you can miss an awful lot of life if you don't have someone important to share it with.

I've really only been in love three times. I guess you could say I've fallen into the magic three times. They fill my head. They have fulfilled my heart.

In the old days, a woman who wanted to attract a man would stitch a sampler and hang it on the wall. It was an audition, a demonstration of skill. Why? Because men understood that the woman they chose would determine their quality of life. Marry a bad seamstress and wear lousy shirts for life. There was a dependency that ran through the entire family. Well, we're not pioneers on the prairie anymore.

There is a substantial service economy out there ready to take care of just about any need. So, what do we need from each other? I think it is emotional support.

What kind of package are you selling? Cute? Funny? Smart?

Capable? Friendly? All of the above? Yes, you are selling it. Why not? People looking for people is the ultimate buyer's market. Are you selling emotional support?

I've noticed that people tend to marry their opposites the first time around. The gregarious man and his quiet wife. The high strung wife and the steady husband. The partier and the let's-go-home-already mate. The second time around you see more people who match their similarities than their differences. It's a different kind of partnership.

It can come from nowhere. You've been best friends for years and now he wants a date. A date date. This happens, you know. When you start losing people at an older age, you just naturally turn to the people you know.

Relationships are important at every age. The odd thing about relationships when you are older is that you understand you have more time. You can get in slowly. I don't think you really know a man until you have spent a year of holidays with him. Watch the way he behaves at Christmas, Valentine's Day, all of them. What is his sense of family? Where does he put you? How does he react to you?

Does he have kids? Does he have kids in jail? How does he treat them? What do they think of you? Does he want you to make biscuits just like his mother did? Or his first wife? Is he jealous? Is he controlling? These are things you know to look for. Measuring points. You've been around.

Unless you are lonely and vulnerable (uh, oh! little brain!) then it is too easy to ignore the questions you know you should answer. Is he broke? Does he just want a nurse? Is he after your money? Is he after your Monet? Is he just waiting for you to croak?

If you are going to remarry, write up the divorce papers while everything is peachy. Put them in a drawer and pray they never come out. Look for a friend instead of a mate and you'll probably never use those papers. Oh, and put the Monet in the pre-nup. Use your Big Brain.

You need to be treated in the way you expect to be treated. You need to be treated like a lady. There's the L word again! If you find yourself with a man who doesn't understand the whole Lady & Gent thing, it's time for a reassessment. Don't settle.

Your maternal clock isn't ticking. He either rises to your level or he's gone. The question is, how? Is he a Fixer-Upper? Do you want to invest yourself in the project. After he's Fixed-Up, what have you really got?

Here is the big question. Does he understand love? No, that's not it. Try this: Does he understand love in the way that you do? It's pretty simple. If love is a Big Brain activity for you and a little brain activity for him…time for another man!

One of my oldest, dearest friends swore she wasn't in love.

I said, "You want to spend time with him?"
She said, "Yes."

I said, "You worry about him?"
She said, "Yes."

I said, "You think about him?"
She said, "Yes."

I said, "You admire and respect him?"
She said, "Yes

I said, "You laugh together?"
She said, "Yes."

I said, "You want to talk, talk, talk?"
She said, "Yes."

I said, "Marcia, what do you think love is?"

You could almost see her Big Brain swinging into action.

Maybe you've noticed that the word "bed" hasn't appeared in this chapter, yet. Okay, here we go . . .

New to you doesn't make it new.

Sex complicates everything. Duh. Don't make it more complicated. If you are 50 do not, *do not* start believing you can behave like a 25-year-old. First off, they may not even be behaving the way you think they are. Is the "hook up" culture of casual sex even real? Is it a media myth? Or is it just a Roman Candle moment of hedonism in youth?

A friend once described college as Sex Camp. Don't go to Sex Camp. Don't even be a counselor. Don't follow your little brain.

You're 50 and you've been out of the dating scene since you were 25. Maybe you never dated. You went from being a daughter directly into being a wife. Either way, you don't have to do things their way. Who is they? They is anybody who isn't you. You are in charge. You are the captain of your ship.

Some things just don't change. Self-worth is still self-worth. I have a friend who says no man spends time with a woman he doesn't want to take to bed. Hmmm. Let's say that's true. So what? That's just what he wants. It doesn't have to be what he gets. Buying you a dinner doesn't buy him a pillow. If you show up on your first date with your toothbrush, that's your decision, but ask yourself, "Then what?"

It's the same in life, isn't it? The groups change. The social structures change. You don't have to. The Road to Special is always there. It's just a matter of whether you are on it or off it.

Kids don't need a dozen "uncles."

You have obligations. You have baggage. Used to be, sex was complicated because you might end up with a child. If you are 50 or 75, it's complicated because you probably already have children.

If every guy you share dinner with in the evening shares pancakes with your kids the next morning, something is wrong.

Use your head, missy. The same things that make you uncomfortable as a parent will make your kids uncomfortable with you. You should behave in the way you expect your children to behave, especially if they are adults.

Translation: Don't sleep with a man who isn't your husband under the same roof with your children, even if your children are adults. They can imagine what they imagine about what you do when they aren't around. You don't have to show them.

I was once in this position. For all those wonderful fifteen years when I was with Tom in Nashville, we never shared a room when his kids or my mother were with us.

Time pays you back if you have class.

I think my generation still works. I think it's because of the rituals. I think the rituals are classy. I'm talking about all the little things.

Hold my chair.
Open my door (yes, I know I can do it myself).
Refresh my drink.
Know how to make an introduction.
Know the art of conversation.

Each one of these says to the people around you, "I honor you."

And so, some final thoughts on age . . .

You really can't be crotchety and classy at the same time. Old and crotchety is just another way of saying selfish. But hey, if you want to go out complaining, go ahead. Just don't start thinking that anybody is listening.

Classy is another way of saying *generous.* The things that make you classy all involve the ways you treat other people. There is really no such thing as old and classy. There is just classy.

Classy is built into the Rituals. There is a generous spirit to the Rituals. They allow you to search for what you like and appreciate in another person.

It would be nice to see more classy nowadays. It's very hard for me to imagine an old couple in rocking chairs, holding hands and listening to *rap*. She gazes at him and says, "Honey, they're playing our song." Thumpa thumpa thumpa.

When I think about age and being classy, I picture my grandmother. I still drink tea from the cup she used to read my tea leaves in when I was a child. What beautiful moments! However, I don't think she drank tea from that cup. Sometimes in the evenings she would say, "Jim and I are having a nice little one." Jim was Jim Beam.

MARY ANN'S TERRIBLE TOO'S

Too outdated
Too passe

Too old fashioned
Too set in your ways
Too unadventurous
Too insecure
Too ambiguous
Too narrow minded
Too inactive
Too out of touch

Illustration by James Bennett

Mother and daughter during the holidays. Photo: Dawn Wells Archives

culmination

fi•na•le

noun

: the last part of something
(such as a musical peformance,
play, etc.)

windup

COMPLETION

LAST ACT

CONCLUSION

FINISH

END

finit

...and that's a wrap

The most beautiful people we have known are those who have known defeat, known suffering, known struggle, known loss, and have found their way out of the depths. These persons have an appreciation, a sensitivity and an understanding of life that fills them with compassion, gentleness, and a deep loving concern. Beautiful people do not just happen.

— Elizabeth Kubler Ross

As much as anything else, this book asks the question, "What will you do with your life?" Will you give it meaning? Will the meaning grow with age? Will you make it special?

What is the first step toward giving meaning to your life, the first step on the Road to Special? To me, it is gratitude.

Without gratitude, you can't stand in awe of the gift of life. Without gratitude, you can't marvel at the world, the universe that surrounds you. Without gratitude, you might start believing those blessings you count are created by . . . *you*. Oh, what a mistake.

You will never stay on the Road to Special if you take the road for granted. You won't even get on the road. *"Beautiful people do not just happen."*

The moment you understand this can be the moment you put every tool we've talked about to good use — perseverance, optimism, manners, work ethic — and build the special person you can be.

It only gets better from there. You now have a foundation for a personal style, a way of being, that burnishes your life — a style that demonstrates *you know what you are doing and why.*

So many times in this book, I have told you that you are on your own. Up until this point, these have been warnings, caution flags, so to speak. Now, though, you are on your own in a far different, and good, way. You are *yourself* on the Road to Special.

What do you want your epitaph to be?

Does the question sound strange? Well, I think the end of a book is a good place to ask it. What will it be? I think you need to know. Why? Because you are writing it right now, today.

Okay, let's say you've "lost a little humanity" and you don't have a back button. How to regain it? Engage your forward button.

Start here and now.
You are the captain of your ship.
Put a little old fashioned Mary Ann in your life.

No matter what condition you were born into. No matter what condition you may have put yourself into, you can still right the course. It is your choice.

You can put the bad stuff behind you.
You can be the master of your condition.
Treat yourself the way you want to be treated.
Treat others that way, too.
Love yourself.

236

Respect your body.
Write down the values you want to live by.
Make those values your best friends.
Make them yours.
If you have self-respect you can never be brought down.
You will never go wrong by doing the right thing.

You will find that you are building a new Rest of Your Life. This is how you will be remembered. Here are top ten things I would like to be remembered as:

Kind. Thoughtful. Generous. Happy. Positive. Optimistic. Sensitive. Smart. Inquisitive. Curious. Opinionated. Strong. Loving. Selective. Challenging. Gentle. Sweet. Seductive . . . Hot.

That's nineteen. Okay, I will never be remembered as "mathematical."

Write what you think your epitaph should be. Now, put it somewhere visible — a place you see every day. Let it inspire you. The day may come when you will want to rewrite it. That may happen many times. Fine. Just keep the old ones. Read them somewhere down the Road to Special and watch yourself grow.

The final Ginger or Mary Ann question.

If you want to consider the Ginger or Mary Ann question in a new way, perhaps project a future for them. After they get off the island, then what?

My guess is that Ginger would return to Hollywood and resume playing . . . Ginger. She'd play that role until she aged and the music stopped.

Mary Ann was a Midwestern girl when she got on the island. In the America of 1964, this meant she was already five years behind the lifestyle in California. So, she was behind the times even before she got marooned.

After getting off the island, she would jump back into life but keep her code. She would discover the brand new women's liberation movement and the brand new birth control pill the minute she stepped back on shore.

It wouldn't faze her. There would be no bra burning for her. Who knows where she could end up. Back in Kansas? In a city? It really doesn't matter.

Wherever she landed, she would contribute. It could be the PTA. It could be the mayor's office.

She would contribute to society.
She would enhance her surroundings.
She would be an asset.
She would be a complete woman.
She would certainly entertain marriage and a family.
She would be a good partner, mother, and companion.
She would enhance any community where she resided.

Whatever goal she set, she would accomplish it. She would be full of passion toward everything she approached and she would be a fabulous, uninhibited lover.

POSTS FROM FACEBOOK

"In elementary school I was a slow learner. Students, teachers, my parents were very mean and cruel to me. My parents beat me. My childhood was a nightmare.

"I would come home from school. I had 30 minutes or so before my parents got home. I would watch *Gilligan's Island*. It made me feel normal and it had special healing powers after surviving a terrible day in school or a night of not waking up in the emergency room at the hospital.

"I used to pray that I would die in my sleep or wish I had the courage to run away to escape this life that I had. *Gilligan's Island* helped me a lot to survive my childhood.

"I haven't seen shows like *Gilligan's Island, I Dream of Jeannie,* or even a *Bugs Bunny* cartoon in years. I really miss those shows. The shows on TV now are not acceptable for any child to watch.

"TV shows back then sold HOPE from reality. Forget your current problems and visit a world of make believe, entertains you if only just for a few minutes. Fills your body with good if only just for a little bit. Thank you for filling my childhood with one good memory."

Friend post on the Dawn Wells Facebook page, 2013

It won't be easy to remake *Gilligan's Island* in the manner that Sherwood intended. Mary Ann was a virgin. Casting will be difficult.

What would Mary Ann do?

Would she be a wife?
Would she be ambitious?
Would she be a good mother?
Would she be a politician?
Would she be an executive?

What would Mary Ann do? You tell me . . . www.dawn-wells.com and facebook.com/therealmaryann.

THE END

The day I finished the last pages of this book,

I found out that we lost Russell Johnson. I

thought of a quote from, of all people, Dr. Seuss:

"Don't cry because it's over.

Smile because it happened."

. . . and then this from Carl Sandburg:

"Life is like an onion.

You peel off one layer at time.

Sometimes you cry."

— Love, "The Rest"

WHAT WOULD MARY ANN DO?

recognition

thanks

noun

: a grateful feeling or acknowledgment of a benefit, favor, or the like, expressed by words or otherwise

thank you

much obliged

GRATITUDE

ACKNOWLEDGMENT

note

merci

Acknowledgments

This book would not be possible without talent and energy of many, many people. This has been a joyous ride.

Rick Rinehart, thank you for trusting the topic and for seeing the value of "the character" that has sustained for more than three generations and is loved worldwide, and for allowing me to express my love and gratitude for *our* Mary Ann.

A special thanks to Steve Stinson. What fun! I thank you for your talent, humor, wisdom, and your creative design of the book. "You got me!" It has been a wonderful collaboration. I learned so much. I thank and appreciate you from the bottom of my heart. It certainly was a rough road until I finally found you. We did it! I know it wasn't easy.

Thanks to Leonard Carter, my manager, who brought us all together. Thank you for providing me with a place to write in your family cabin in the wonderful Blue Ridge Mountains. Thanks for encouraging me and caring for me. Thank you for good constructive input and criticism. A personal thank you for your talent and insight and partnership and seeing the book through to its final hour. And your smile.

Applause to Jim Bennett, illustrator extraordinaire, for your illustrations of our "Mary Ann's Terrible Too's." What a delight. I am so honored.

To Sherwood Schwartz, thank you for the creation of Mary Ann and giving her to me to bring to life.

Thanks to Julia Flint and Robert Rauch for keeping me on track and enduring long hours with a positive attitude.

Thanks to Brett Kloepfer. I thank you for beginning the journey with me through the ever-changing process and helping me overcome the obstacles along the way.

Thanks to Fred Westbrook, my agent and supporter for more than thirty years, with my career and with this book. You're a champ and a marvel. You believe in me.

And, finally, thanks to Harlan Boll of BHBPR, my trusted publicist, for your incredible insight and talent.

— Dawn

There is so much more to **Dawn Wells** than Mary Ann of *Gilligan's Island* (the longest running sitcom still showing worldwide in over 30 languages)!

She's an actress, producer, author, spokesperson, journalist, motivational speaker, teacher, and chairwoman of the Terry Lee Wells Foundation — focusing on women and children in northern Nevada.

She has starred in more than 150 TV shows, and seven motion pictures, including *Winterhawk* (which she also narrated), *The Town That Dreaded Sundown* (with Andrew Prine), *Super Sucker* (with Jeff Daniels), *The New Interns, It's Our Time,* and most recently, *Silent But Deadly.*

She has starred in more than 60 theatrical productions, from Noel Coward to Neil Simon, as well as the National Tours of *Chapter Two* and *They're Playing Our Song.* Favorite productions include *Fatal Attraction* with Ken Howard, *The Odd Couple* with Marcia Wallace, *The Allergist's Wife, Steel Magnolias* (Ouiser), and *The Vagina Monologues.*

Dawn has starred as Gingy in *Love, Loss, and What I Wore* (by Nora and Delia Ephron) in New York, Chicago, Delaware, Scottsdale, and San Jose.

She was the "castaway correspondent" for Channel 9 (Sydney, Australia) interviewing actors and directors such as Robin Williams, Eddie Murphy, Julia Roberts, Rene Russo, Mel Gibson, Ron Howard, and Richard Donner.

As a producer, she brought two Movies of the Week to CBS: *Surviving Gilligan's Island* and *Return To The Bat Cave,* with Adam West. She ran her Film Actors Boot Camp for seven years in Idaho.

•••

Steve Stinson is an artist and writer in Virginia, where he lives with his patient wife in the world's smallest five-bedroom house. When he was young and limber, he was a juggler and wrote comic strips. Today, his grandchildren call him "Bebop." His four children's books — *Grumpypants, Where Kent Went, Darien the Crustatarien,* and *My Favorite Nursery Rhymes* — will be classics someday.